The
NETZERETH
TRIAL

Rick Drost

The Netzereth Trial

Copyright © 2024 Rick Drost

ISBN (Paperback): 978-1-964494-69-2
ISBN (Ebook): 978-1-964494-70-8

Printed in the United States of America.

PROMINENT
BOOKS

5830 E 2nd St, Ste 7000 #9983
Casper, WY 82609
USA

Olive branch clip art by OpenClipart-Vectors

Netzer: n. a young branch or shoot that grows from the trunk or roots of a tree, commonly seen in olive trees

Isaiah 11:1–5, 10
A shoot (netzer) will come up from the stump of Jesse;
from his roots a Branch will bear fruit.
² The Spirit of the LORD will rest on him—
the Spirit of wisdom and of understanding,
the Spirit of counsel and of might,
the Spirit of the knowledge and fear of the LORD—
³ and he will delight in the fear of the LORD.
He will not judge by what he sees with his eyes,
or decide by what he hears with his ears;
⁴ but with righteousness he will judge the needy,
with justice he will give decisions for the poor of the earth.
He will strike the earth with the rod of his mouth;
with the breath of his lips he will slay the wicked.
⁵ Righteousness will be his belt
and faithfulness the sash around his waist.
**¹⁰ In that day the Root of Jesse will stand
as a banner for the peoples;
the nations will rally to him, and his
resting place will be glorious.**

INTRO

James received the news from the Jerusalem messenger, and his mouth fell open. The events of the past week had completely changed the way he understood the world. His family had been ripped apart by ideologies and misunderstandings. His friendship with a true companion had been stretched to the limit and then destroyed. His beliefs about his brother had been tested, failed, reborn, and now dashed again. His heart could not take one more vicious stab. It was a wonder that he had any hope left at all. And yet, if he understood the significance it could set things right again. That is, if the message were true...

CHAPTER 1

It's the fourth day already, Hadassah thought as she let go a deep sigh and turned to the wooden table to roll out another sheet of unleavened bread. "I have too much to do before tomorrow, Sarah. Do you think we could ask the Almighty to stop time for mommy?"

Sarah turned her little head, smiled, and peaked her eyebrows when she heard her name. But she quickly returned her attention to the small straw doll in her lap, so Hadassah continued with her work.

Hadassah wiped the sweat from her brow and looked up at the trees that grew just outside the walls of her home's compound. It was a beautiful day but there was not even the hint of a breeze in the trees. Usually working in the courtyard during the springtime in Netzereth you could count on cool weather and cloudy skies. And although Hadassah had started the day thanking the Almighty that it wasn't raining, she would now welcome a slight drizzle to break the heat of the morning sun.

The family of James lived on a spacious lot in the town of Netzereth. Most common Israelite homes were one room single story structures with a courtyard where most of the living of the inhabitants took place. James' family enjoyed a larger than usual home primarily because of the profession of the family as carpenters and stone masons. Their courtyard was surrounded by a wall which encompassed three, soon to be four, free standing rooms. The wall had a large gate that led to the street and the rest of Netzereth, and a small gate that led to a family garden and small stable.

"Eema." Hadassah heard the inquisitive shout come from the garden gate where she had sent her five-year-old son to fetch some fresh herbs.

"Did you remember to bring some parsley, Joshua?"

"Eema, come here."

"Joshua, I'm very busy. Just open the gate and bring me the herbs." After a short pause and her son's continuous calls, she placed her rolling pin on the table and limped to the garden gate that led out of the courtyard. "Joshua, what's wrong?"

"I can't open the gate."

She pushed open the gate and quickly relieved her son of some of his load. "Sorry dear, I didn't need you to get so much, but thank you for your help." She added under her breath, "I can use all the help I can get."

After placing the herbs on the table, she bent down and picked up Sarah and patted the limestone dust off her bottom. "Joshua, did you check on the Passover Lamb as I asked?"

"Eema, will uncle be here for Passover?" Joshua looked at her with pleading eyes.

"All your uncles will be h… oh you mean Uncle Jesus?" She pulled his head to her side and gave him a hug. "Honey, I know you want to see him more often, but he spends his Passovers in Jerusalem. And your uncle is um… very busy."

"But why don't we go to Jerusalem for Passover also?" Joshua asked with excitement. "We could see Uncle then, couldn't we?"

Hadassah gave a big sigh as she thought about how to answer Joshua. "Yes, it would be great to see your Uncle Jesus again but I'm afraid it's just not possible this Passover, son. It takes almost a whole week to travel to Jerusalem from here. Don't you remember the long trip we took a couple months ago for Sukkot? We traveled with most of the village. And it was decided with many of the Netzerim that we would stay home this Passover and make the trip next year for Passover. Remember, you were so tired from the traveling that you fell asleep as Abba and your uncles built our tent on the Mount of Olives? Passover is just two days away. I'm sorry, we can't go this year." Then wishing to change the subject Hadassah asked, "Did you check on the lamb?"

"Yes Eema. I checked him for scrapes." He continued to look at her with pleading, deep brown eyes.

Just then, there was a call at the front gate. "Hadassah, would you care for some company this morning?" Emma, Hadassah's best friend, charged into the homestead's court-yard uninvited.

Emma and her husband Jacob owned a small textile shop. They sold cloth from all over the Roman Empire, which required Jacob to travel often to Caesarea and Tyre to purchase goods from the merchant ships. That fact left the gregarious Emma in charge of the shop for days on end. Her outspoken, jovial attitude proved to be fortunate for the shop in the past two years of financial ostracizing. Not many people could resist Emma's charm even if she was heretical in her belief concerning Jesus of Netzereth.

"Shouldn't you be at home getting ready for the Passover or watching the store?" Hadassah said with a smile. Hadassah's two children screamed with delight at the appearance of Emma. Joshua ran headlong into Emma's left leg and gave it a bear hug.

Emma tussled Joshua's dark hair and smiled at him as she spoke to Hadassah. "The store is fine without me today. Jacob came home yesterday from Caesarea. We have had no business and he had some stocking to do of the new cloth he bought at the docks. So, we closed for the day. Everyone's too busy today anyway. Our type of business might as well take a three-day holiday when preparation day, Passover, and the Sabbath are so close together. I thought I would come over and see if you needed any help."

"Thank you! I could really use it. Joshua keeps interrupting me with his constant questions about Passover. And little Sarah" she said pecking her thirteen-month-old's cheek, "keeps getting into all the limestone dust making the areas I have already cleaned dirty again!"

"Well, as the children get older they will be of more help and your work will be a bit easier." Emma smiled as she looked at little Sarah who indeed was covered in dust.

"Only if they grow to be as responsible as your boy, Jesse," Hadassah said. "I suppose he is helping Jacob in the shop today?"

"Yes he is, but they are almost done and I told Jesse to come over here to watch your two angels while we work." Emma smiled softly and strolled over to the worktable in the center of the courtyard.

Hadassah would never have asked Emma for the help she desperately needed, even though the home of James and Hadassah was by far the grandest home in the small village of Netzereth and she was the only adult female to prepare it for special occasions. And she was about to protest, when Emma asked, "So what have you accomplished so far?"

"Well, since the great room is being used mainly for storage or the odd meal during bad weather, it has long been set and ready for the Passover meal. James' mother is seldom here to sleep in her room." Looking to the west of the great room, Hadassah continued. "I have also finished sweeping out our room and hopefully Joshua and Sarah can leave it that way."

"That is such a lovely room." Emma interrupted Hadassah's listing of completed tasks. "I am surprised the building of your room didn't take twice as long as it did."

"Oh, I know! I am still enthralled with the room James prepared for me. It is half the size of the great room but the art of the stonework both inside and outside is so beautiful."

Emma walked over to James' and Hadassah's room as she said, "Obviously James put a lot of love into building this home for the two of you." She lovingly ran her hand over some of the geometric designs chiseled into a limestone pillar near the doorway. "It sure is a work of art. Even the ceiling and floor show your husband's flare for beauty... and love for you."

Emma's words about Hadassah's relationship with James caused Hadassah some discomfort and she looked away to hide her feelings. Mercifully, Emma continued the verbal list Hadassah had started. "Did you remember to clean the stairway and roof?"

On the outer north wall of Hadassah's room, a basalt stairway with a beautiful olive wood handrail led to the roof of their home. The sturdy roof became home for the family during the feast of Tabernacles. All Jews enjoyed celebrating the festival by constructing shelters on the roofs of their homes to commemorate how their ancestors lived in tents during the forty years of wandering in the wilderness.

"That was the first place I cleaned." Hadassah responded. "The view from the roof always takes my breath away. From there I can look over the whole Esdraelon plain. It is especially beautiful during the growing season when fields of barley sway in the wind."

"Oh Hadassah, I love the view you have of the hills of Samaria."

Hadassah nodded in enthusiastic agreement, "Those green hills are full of flocks of doves. I often go up to the roof and stare at those hills. I daydream about walking through the woods, scaring up the birds to flight, and hearing the beating of their wings as they make their escape." Hadassah's tone revealed a deep longing.

"Why don't you go and do that some day?" Emma asked.

"Emma, you know perfectly well we are not allowed to cross into Samaritan land. Any dealing with Gentiles, Samaritans, and sinners is strictly forbidden by the teachings of the Netzerim. And besides," she added, "my foot prevents me from traveling long distances."

"I know someone who could take care of both of those excuses for you." Emma cocked her head and looked at Hadassah with a smile. Hadassah immediately recognized the sly attempt to stir up Emma's favorite conversation.

"Emma," Hadassah conceded with a plaintive sigh, "you know I love Jesus dearly and He already saved me once, but... it's complicated."

"But Hadassah, you are still the pearl."

"Emma, you rascal." Hadassah said with a smile.

The word pearl caught the attention of Joshua, and a big grin came to the face of Emma.

"Eema, please tell me the plearl story. Please, please."

Hadassah gave Emma a knowing grin and a sigh. "Emma, you know I have so much work to complete."

"Yes, but the children need some eema time too." Emma displayed her infectious grin and Hadassah relented.

This was Joshua's favorite story. And honestly, it was Hadassah's favorite also. She sat down with Sarah in her lap. Emma had already placed Joshua on her knees and sat opposite Hadassah, where the two of them waited to hear the story again.

Hadassah began, "I had despaired of ever marrying. But then everything changed when a very handsome man of marrying age approached my father and asked about me. His name was Jesus."

Joshua leaned off Emma's lap to get closer to his mother. "That's daddy's big brother, huh eema?"

"Yes, honey, and he was looking for a wife for your abba."

"I have the same name don't I eema?"

"Yes, but we call you by your Hebrew name, Joshua. We named you after your uncle Jesus because we love Him and we want you to grow up to be like Him." The last few words of that sentence caught in Hadassah's throat. But Hadassah recovered quickly and continued, "Now, please let me tell the story without so many questions. Okay, son?"

Joshua nodded and settled back in Emma's lap. Hadassah continued, "I listened just outside the door wanting to hear the conversation of Jesus and my father. Jesus asked, 'Is the beautiful young lady I saw in the marketplace promised to anyone yet?'

"That was you, huh eema?"

Hadassah nodded, raised her eyebrows to signal her son to remain silent, and continued with the story. "Jesus demonstrated genuine surprise when my father said no one had spoken for me yet. Actually, several other men had inquired about marrying me but they all backed out when they learned the truth about my deformity. I felt rejected and humiliated every time it happened. I hated this whole process." Hadassah paused, lost in painful thoughts. She recovered with a sudden start. "But I'm getting ahead of the story."

"The bride price and dowry were then discussed. As usual, my father offered a dowry larger than the last time in hopes of making the marriage covenant. I expected Jesus to offer a low bride price. I was, after all, eighteen already, almost an old maid. The price I heard however was very generous. It was in fact the price my first suitor six years earlier had offered. That offer, and every one since, had fallen through as soon as they learned of my problem. I could tell that my father was excited about Jesus' offer but was also carefully checking his emotions. He was always a good negotiator in his business but this was different because I was his 'pearl'." Hadassah smiled as Joshua brightened and opened his mouth to interrupt with another question, but he choked it down when she put her finger to her lips.

"The conversation lasted the whole day as my father inquired about Jesus' family and their ability to care for his 'pearl'. Jesus also asked questions of my father but not the usual kind. He seemed to be more concerned with my family's needs than our lineage or social stature. He had even jokingly said" Hadassah deepened her voice to sound more masculine, "'the Almighty could make children of Abraham out of these cups'. The fact that my family was not in the line of David, but instead of Benjamin didn't seem to bother him at all!"

Joshua couldn't contain himself any longer. "Talk about the plearl, eema!"

Hadassah smiled, "Finally the moment came when I was to walk out and stand before Jesus in my best outfit and impress him with my beauty and worth by serving him and my father a meal I had prepared. I tried to hide my limp as I served them but it was still very obvious. As I worked, Jesus' eyes grew big and a look of shock came over his face. I knew once again that I had failed the test. Jesus stood from the table and approached me. I trembled with disappointment and hurt as he put his hand on my shoulder." Hadassah's eyes moistened as she relived the memory.

"It's okay eema, I love you."

"You are such an insightful child, Joshua." And then turning to Hadassah, Emma added, "I think he will grow up to be like his uncle."

"Okay, both of you let me finish the story." She took a deep breath and blinked away the tears. "My father said to Jesus, 'She has a slight problem with her right foot. She has since birth.' Jesus continued to stare into my eyes and took my hands in his. I didn't want to look at him. I was so embarrassed! I had failed again to impress the family of a suitor. I was worthless. I would be an old maid forever. After a pause that seemed ages long, my father said, 'Do you wish to adjust the bride price?'"

"'Of course I do!' Jesus replied, 'I increase it by 50 shekels. You underestimate the value of your daughter sir. She is truly as you say, 'a pearl,' a pearl of great price!'"

"Is that true mommy?"

"Every word of it, my little schmeeka." Hadassah replied using the pet name she had for her son.

Joshua hopped off Emma's lap and began skipping around the courtyard. "My eema is the plearl of price and I'm a little schmeeka."

Hadassah looked at Emma and admitted, "I fell in love with Jesus at that point but it was his brother I was promised to wed. In the three years it took James to prepare a place for me, I began to love everyone in this family. After the wedding feast James showed me the new room he had built for us. He pointed out the exquisite detail and love he put into that room for me. I never had second thoughts about my love for James. And I have never lost my love for Jesus. He was the first, outside of my family, who truly showed love for me. But Emma, when Jesus left the Netzerim to become a Pharisee he hurt his whole family and this whole town! I know Jesus could heal my foot. And I'm sure you believe that cavorting with Samaritans is permissible, but the pain of Jesus' betrayal is too deep," then she added softly, "even though I love him so."

Emma replied, "I know he loves all of you as well. And he hurts just as you do about the separation that has occurred in your family. Jacob and I heard one of his teachings once when he spoke of the sword that will divide families because of commitment to following the Almighty. Jesus, James, and the rest of the family have lived this division he spoke of. And I could hear the pain in his voice as he quoted the prophet Micah, 'I have come to turn a man against his father, a daughter against her mother, a daughter-in-law against her mother-in-law, a man's enemies will be the members of his own household.'

Hadassah looked at Emma with misty eyes. "That's a great description of the problem. But what is the solution?"

"I'm not sure Hadassah, but I think we will know soon. Jesus is spending more time in Jerusalem and He will surely announce His claim to the throne of David in Jerusalem. When that happens everything will become clear."

"I hope you are right, but it is exactly that claim that brings the division! This division between James and Jesus is hard for me to bear." Hadassah paused in thought and then suddenly exclaimed with a shake of her head, "But let's not talk of this now. I have many things to do before James comes home. Where were we before we were sidetracked by your clever mention of the pearl?" The twinkle in Hadassah's large brown eyes returned and she playfully slapped Emma's shoulder.

Emma chuckled, "I'm sorry. I love hearing that story and I know Joshua likes it too. You were saying that the two main rooms are done. How about the boys' room?" She pointed with her head to the other side of the courtyard as she got to her feet and took Sarah from Hadassah.

"Oh, that is their problem." Hadassah said as both women stood and took a few steps toward the room. "They are old enough to clean up their own room. But I'm sure there is no leaven in there. They are hardly home long enough to eat. And they never eat in that room. It was originally built as a workroom for father Joseph's masonry work. It is full of tools that Joseph Jr. uses for his apprenticeship with James. It also has Judas' parchments for his scribe work with Isaiah, and Simon's metal work tools. So it is still mainly a storage room which the brothers use to get away from the children." Hadassah smirked knowing full well that the brothers of James would deny that description of them.

"Simon does excellent work, Hadassah! Tell him I love the knives he made for me."

"Yes, I don't complain too much about Simon's things. The cooking utensils I have are the best in the village. Look at that ladle on the table. He made that for me. Isn't it beautiful?"

Returning their attention to the cooking, Hadassah continued to work the dough she had been rolling out when Emma arrived. Emma set Sarah down with her doll and picked up the variety of herbs that Joshua had brought from the garden and began cutting them.

"The boy's room is their room; they must clean the inside. I just need to get their tools that are spilling out the door back in there." Hadassah continued. "My main concern is the room that Joseph is preparing for Zerah, his betrothed. Joseph works on the room every night except the Sabbath and holy days. He is anxious to marry and James has to slow him down constantly to ensure the quality of the workman-ship. James tells him often, "A new bride will not live inside drafty walls or under a leaky roof." So Joseph works, James critiques, and the walls slowly grow." Huffing, she added,

"And the loose rock, limestone dust, and general mess make keeping this home clean, a terrible chore."

A call at the front double gated entrance turned their heads and Jesse, Emma's twelve-year-old son, came through and bent to tickle Joshua who had run to him. "I'm here mother. What needs to be done?"

"If you could just watch the children for us that would be great! Thank you son."

"Yes, thank you Jesse. If you want, you can take them down to the stable and check on the lamb." Hadassah added.

Jesse picked up Sarah and led Joshua through the narrow garden gate that began a path to a family cave. The cave had many uses through the years. Right now it stabled the lamb that was to be slain for the Passover.

With Sarah and Joshua out of the way, the two women busied themselves for the rest of the afternoon, accomplishing a variety of tasks in comfortable camaraderie. "Emma, could you please pull the bread out of the oven?"

"Why are you baking so much bread?" Emma placed two newly baked loaves on the table next to a basket full of unleavened bread.

"Remember, there are four grown men to feed in this family, and my experience with Passover is that they will each eat more than their share. Also I am baking some for Isaiah and his new apprentice, Matthan, for their meal." Then Hadassah added with a chuckle, "So be careful how you handle that bread."

"That young man needs to put on a happy face." Emma quipped. "Each day has enough worry for its own, yet he seems to want to worry about everyone's business for the whole week. He scares me sometimes too. The other day Matthan came into the shop, supposedly to buy some material for a new tunic, but I was sure he was looking for some reason to declare us unclean. Leprosy on my son would have brought a smile to his face."

"Emma, he's not that bad. Every new apprentice needs to show off his knowledge a little. He'll mellow with time."

"I hope you're right, but it would be nice if he smiled occasionally. Now Isaiah, he knows how to have a good time. I enjoy his teaching in the synagogue. He comes up with the most humorous statements. And it seems to come so naturally for him, but maybe he sits up late at night thinking up his one-liners." Emma paused a second as she rearranged the unleavened bread she had just removed from the oven. "Jesus, on the other hand, enlightens me when he teaches. It's like being in a dark room looking for a piece of cloth that you know is there and only when you bring in a lamp does it turn out to be right in front of you. Jesus is that lamp. The life I always knew was there in the law and prophets but couldn't see, is suddenly right in front of me when Jesus teaches."

Hadassah interrupted, "Let's not talk of Jesus right now. James will be home soon."

No sooner had the words left her mouth when James walked through the front gate.

"Hadassah," James bellowed without looking as he entered. "Bring me my tools please."

"No need to shout I'm right here. You aren't going to work on that filthy thing today are you?" The "thing" was a limestone pillar which stood in the corner of the courtyard.

"I have to finish it soon, wife. I just heard on my way home through the marketplace that a meeting of the elders has been called tonight. I'm sure Isaiah wants to know when this final pillar will be done for the new synagogue porch." James removed his outer cloak and began sizing up the work yet to be done on the pillar. "Honestly, I think he envisions himself sitting in the shade of the porch dispensing his wisdom to all the Netzerim like Solomon." He chuckled at the thought and then turned to see if Hadassah had brought the tools. "Oh, excuse me Emma. I did not realize we had company. Please forgive my rudeness. I get focused sometimes and I forget to take in my surroundings. And please don't mention what I just said about Isaiah to anyone. You know I love the man."

"No need to apologize, James. I think you're right. Isaiah does enjoy the attention his position brings and yet, in some way, it endears us to him. Hopefully some of his good-natured spirit will rub off on his young apprentice."

"Who? Oh, Matthan, he'll be fine. He's just young and idealistic." James said those last words half-heartedly as he had again turned toward the pillar searching for his next project.

"Here are your tools, husband. Please don't stir up too much dust. Emma and I are just finishing the baking and no one enjoys limestone flavored unleavened bread for Passover!" Hadassah gave James a peck on the cheek and set the toolbox at his feet.

"Woman. We have a guest. Don't be so forward."

"I'm sorry sir." Hadassah replied with mock seriousness. This was a favorite game that they often played in front others in town. Many in Netzereth were accustomed to their demonstrations of love, but few appreciated it as Emma did. Whereas most wives followed their husbands through town when they traveled together, James and Hadassah walked side by side talking together. It was scandalous.

Emma whispered to Hadassah as they turned back to their work, "Do you know how blessed you are? Where did he learn to care for you so?"

"He blames his oldest brother with the lax way he treats me and most women. It's another thing that brings Jesus such ridicule in our society. They say he has no decorum. But," she added in a hushed voice, "I love his lack of decorum."

They both giggled and looked over their shoulders to see if James had overheard. A shout at the gate brought them out of their schoolgirl moods. Hadassah ran to the gate and opened it for a very round man dressed in fine robes and the prayer shawl and headdress of an important teacher of the Torah.

"Welcome Isaiah. My husband is over here working on the pillar…" She let the words trail away as Isaiah was not listening anyway and had already moved over next to James.

"James, this is coming along nicely. But come my son, we must talk." Isaiah led James to a corner of the courtyard removed from the women.

"I know you want this pillar finished soon, and it will be, but I must make sure it is perfect before moving it to it's place on the porch." James would not let anyone hurry his work not even an important man such as Isaiah.

"I know son. That is why you were chosen for this valuable work. The first three pillars are magnificent! And in fact, all the elders are pleased with the swiftness of your work. We realize that this is a labor of love done in your spare time after working hard for the Gentiles in Sepphoris." The last three words came with a bit of harshness that James recognized as a slap on the hand for dealing with those who were not of the Almighty's good favor. But James and Isaiah both knew the necessity of financial dealings with the unclean in order to live. The Roman occupation had made it necessary.

"No James, I come concerning other business. The son of Jonas returned today with distressing news from Jerusalem. You know the boy don't you?" Without waiting for an answer Isaiah continued. "He is a remarkable young man, not unlike your brother, Judas. Good head for learning and the Torah. He was visiting his uncle in the Essene quarter of the Holy City and has just now returned with news of utmost importance. The whole city is in an uproar. The elders and I have decided to call a meeting of the men of Netzereth to discuss how it will affect us here."

"I heard there would be a meeting tonight and I was planning on attending."

"Good, good, my son. It will be very important for you to be there. Your input will help us deal with this issue."

"Why? I mean, why me specifically? I'm no one important in the village."

Isaiah hesitated, appearing to think through a number of wording options.

"Abba." The excited call from Joshua caused both men to look to the far side of the courtyard where Joshua was just emerging from the garden path gate with Jesse behind him carrying Sarah.

"Joshua, show your respect for Rabbi Isaiah."

"Good afternoon Rabbi." Joshua spoke with such reverence, and Isaiah smiled broadly.

He stooped to pick up Joshua and said to James, "You are training your son well." And then looking Joshua in the eye he said, "I would imagine that you are all ready to take your place at Passover tomorrow and ask those very important questions, hmm?"

"Yes sir, 'Why is this bread different? Why is this night different? Why do we eat sour... umm things? Why do we dip the ummm sour things two times? And why are we eating roasted lamb?" Joshua rattled the questions out so fast that Isaiah had to laugh out loud.

"Very good young man! But the "sour things", as you call them, are bitter herbs. You will do well tomorrow, if you don't have everyone rolling on the ground with laughter."

"Bitter herbs, bitter herbs." Joshua repeated the phrase over and over as Isaiah lowered him to the ground.

"Joshua, run along to your mother." James ordered, and then turning to Rabbi Isaiah, asked again, "Why is my presence important at the meeting tonight?"

"It concerns your brother, Jesus. He will bring us all to ruin if he is not stopped."

CHAPTER 2

(Wednesday evening)

J ames walked to the synagogue with his brothers. Judas led the way quickly navigating the narrow streets and thickening crowd.

"Slow down Judas. They will not start without us."

Judas swung quickly around and stopped his brothers in their tracks speaking fiercely. "James, if we do not get to the meeting before the roar of debate, we will never be heard. You never take seriously the impact our oldest brother has on this family. If what I have heard is at all true, it may be our turn to be taken to the cliffs of Netzereth."

"You forget who you are Judas. I am still the head of our family. And you are acting like a child." James took a deep breath and softened, "It may be time for concern, but let's not show the assembly our unease as we walk in and thereby set the mood that will lead to the cliffs."

Judas lowered his gaze and nodded. James took the lead and Judas, still fuming, fell in step with his brothers, Joseph and Simon.

The synagogue was half full when they entered. James noticed the elders of Netzereth standing near the dais talking with Nathaniel, the son of Jonas. They were listening again to the news that he had brought from Jerusalem. They stood in a tight group and whispered furtively. In the middle of the group Isaiah commanded the conversation and only occasionally looked to Nathaniel for what must have been clarifying information.

Suddenly the elders broke their huddle and took their seats around the bema in the middle of the assembly. Isaiah ascended the three steps of the bema and stood in front of the other elders. His apprentice Matthan stood at the front of the crowd that had now formed in the synagogue.

Isaiah spoke. "Men of Netzereth, today, Nathaniel, son of Jonas,... I still remember when he read Torah at his bar-mitzvah, and look at him now, a righteous man of King David's line." A ripple of laughter rolled through the room as everyone thought back to a younger Nathaniel. Isaiah continued, "He came from Jerusalem with some very disturbing news. I will let him share in his own words."

A nod to Nathaniel signaled him to ascend the bema. James noticed that Nathaniel avoided eye contact with him and his brothers. However, James could feel the stare of over sixty sets of eyes on the back of his head.

"I was visiting my uncle in the Essene community of Jerusalem last week", Nathaniel began. "On the day after the Sabbath a large crowd gathered on the Mount of Olives. I arrived at the Sheep Gate just in time to see Jesus riding a donkey's foal into Jerusalem to the shouts of the crowd. They were yelling 'Hosanna, Blessed is he who comes in the name of the Almighty.'"

The room erupted with shouts of outrage. Isaiah held up his hands to silence the assembly.

Nathaniel continued, "The crowd was so huge and loud that the Roman garrison was called out of Antonia fortress to patrol the streets. It seemed that everything was coming to a head with the crowd yelling, the army out in force, and the priests in an uproar as Jesus entered the Temple court. Many of his followers wanted to make him king at that moment but he just walked away."

Someone from behind James yelled out, "He is NOT the King of Israel!" Loud discussions started all over the synagogue and Isaiah stepped forward next to Nathaniel.

Judas spoke to his brothers. "This is not going well. You know these people fear a permanent Roman presence here. Jesus is going to be the death of us. The Romans don't tolerate pretenders to the throne."

"Silence, men of Netzereth." Isaiah bellowed above the din. The room quickly calmed and Isaiah continued. "What is happening in Jerusalem is always of importance to the rest of the Jewish people, but we must put everything in perspective. Even we here in Netzereth until a short four years ago believed that Jesus would be the promised Messiah. We know better now. And I am confident that as people really listen to his teaching and observe his disregard for the Law, they will realize that he is an imposter. However, the Romans have never shown patience in dealing with challenges to their authority. And since Netzereth is his hometown, Jesus does bring down the threat of the Roman military on us all. We must be prepared to show the Roman authorities that we as a town do not support the uprising that Jesus' messianic hopes are fanning to flame."

James made a quick search for his good friend Jacob but did not see him in the crowd. He let out a sigh of relief. The words of Isaiah would have opened a barrage of arguments from Jacob and a few other men who still supported Jesus in the village. Obviously none of them had been invited to the assembly.

"The Messiah is the Son of David. Not the son of a whore." The cry came from the back of the room. The room exploded again with shouts from every corner. Simon pulled his brothers close to him and showed them the dagger he had brought with him. James shook his head and motioned to Simon to keep it concealed.

Ezra stood from the seats of elders in front of the bema and quieted the assembly. "Brothers, we will not solve anything with hateful words. Remember that James and his brothers are among us and they have proven themselves to be righteous men also awaiting the Holy Branch from Jesse's line. We are all of David's family. We all know the Scriptures tell us that the Branch, the Messiah, will come from us. We are the chosen. It is unfortunate that one of us has abandoned the way in his self-seeking desire to make a name for himself. But we must not bring shame on his family that has remained true to the principles of Essene living and in particular the Netzerim. No more talk of Jesus' lineage." And then turning to face James and his brothers, Ezra said, "I apologize for the hurt that our words bring you my brothers. Men, you all know how James works tirelessly on this synagogue, and Joseph too. They were taught well by their father before his death. And Judas is showing himself to be a scribe of excellence working with Isaiah and Matthan. In fact, I understand that Judas may even be in line for study and work in the Scriptorium of the wilderness school near the Dead Sea."

The mention of Judas' great honor brought several nodding heads and murmurs of agreement.

Isaiah continued the thought that Ezra had started. "And who has not benefited from the excellent metal work of the youngest son of Joseph, Simon?" The atmosphere of the room cooled as each person thought on the positive influence that James and his brothers had on the village. Isaiah used this calm in the storm to invite James to the bema.

James gave a quick look of caution to his three brothers and ascended the bema. He had been thinking about how to communicate his family's support of the Netzerim, their beliefs, and their way of life to the assembly ever since Isaiah had visited his home earlier in the day. As he began he hoped he had the right words to say.

"Men of Netzereth," James began, "I stand with my brothers as loyal men of the Righteous Way and of the Netzerim. You all know that when our brother moved to

Capernaum and aligned himself with the Pharisee sect, he broke his ties with the Righteous Ones, the Netzerim. And you know that we, his own family, went to speak with him. We told him that he was foolishly abandoning the way of his fathers. That he was recklessly throwing away his heritage, the hopes of his people, and the support of those who had believed in him from the day his birth was foretold."

Murmurs began but James kept speaking in order to quell the known objections to Jesus' birth story.

"You also know that we were unsuccessful in turning him from the path he has chosen. This latest event is disturbing and we, the sons of Joseph, support the elders and men of the Netzerim."

Isaiah stepped forward and put his arm around James. "Brothers, I appreciate James' word to us tonight and I remember the many events that have led us to this night. Perhaps we should have acted with more determination in the past to forestall this night. But really we all must take responsibility for how we have contributed to this threat to our way of life. As a young man newly assigned to the wilderness school I heard with excitement the news of a Netzerim virgin and her vision of the angel Gabriel. I once supported the claims of Joseph and Mary and their insistence of messages from the Almighty that their son was the promised one. You all grew up with him. And although some of his behavior was unusual, most of you fully supported his work and study of the Torah. He was the brightest pupil I have ever had and at his bar mitzvah in the Holy City he even astounded the teachers of the law there. Although we all know the Sad-ducees and their teachers are easy to confound." Laughter ran through the room again as Isaiah's light-hearted way of speaking the truth continued to soften the hearts of those present and allay fears of immediate Roman attack.

"So, as I was saying, we all can take a little responsibility in what has transpired recently. We created the monster and now we must deal with it." Again, some chuckles, but James stepped from the bema with his brow furrowed.

"So now he is a monster?" Joseph asked James when he was close enough to hear the whispered question. "Should we not defend our own flesh and blood?"

James put his hand on the back of Joseph's neck and pulled his brother's head close to his so that their foreheads touched. "The time is not right my brother. Patience."

The head elder, Jeremiah, stood and said, "But we must not act as impatiently as we did last time. It was not well thought through and Jesus escaped our grasp because we were not all unified in our attempt to silence the heretic."

Matthan spoke for the first time. "Excuse my ignorance, Fathers, but I am not aware of an attempt to silence the here-tic Jesus. Can you please share with me the events so I can be better prepared to offer solutions to our present dilemma?"

"I don't like his tone or words." Joseph whispered to his brothers.

Isaiah responded to his apprentice, "Approximately three years ago, Jesus came to Netzereth, and as is custom we invited him to teach on the Sabbath." Matthan gave a quizzical look and his back stiffened. "You must remember, at that time he was still well respected by a great number of Netzerim, even though he had thrown in his lot with the Pharisees. Even the elders were divided in opinion about him." Matthan's stance softened and he nodded.

"The prescribed text for that day was in Isaiah. Still my favorite prophet I might add." He paused to allow the chuckles to dissipate and continued. "I remember that Jesus took the scroll and looked briefly at the passage and then quoted from memory,

'The Spirit of the Lord is on me,
because he has anointed me
to preach good news to the poor.
He has sent me to proclaim freedom for the prisoners
and recovery of sight for the blind,
to release the oppressed,
to proclaim the year of the Lord's favor.'"

All the elders stood with the rest of the assembly as Isaiah himself quoted the passage.

"Jesus then sat and taught us beautifully from the passage. Even I was tempted to overlook his Pharisaical associations and consider again his claim to the throne of David. But then he refused to demonstrate his authority which had been reported in Capernaum. Imagine that. He would not heal anyone in his hometown. He went on to say that we were not worthy of the Almighty's grace. That we, the Netzerim, were less worthy than the gentile dogs which he has since then shown such concern over. He compared us to the Baal worshippers of Elijah's time. He repudiated the blessing that the Almighty has obviously in His Scriptures given to His people Israel and specifically to the descendants of David. He abandoned the faith."

Isaiah's voice rose with each statement. His face turned crimson and his fists flew wildly as he yelled.

Isaiah continued, "As one man the elders determined that his poisonous words must be stopped and with the help of many faithful men we led him to the cliffs at the edge of town. We were about to send him to his death at the base of the cliff when a question arose about the accused person's right to speak in his defense. He already had said enough in my mind, but a new debate began and as we argued Jesus escaped. Through lack of unity, we missed our chance to save the faith."

The assembly in fervor over Isaiah's speech began to call for the death of Jesus. The deafening roar shook the room. Judas tried to say something to James but not a single word reached James' ears. It didn't matter; his expressions spoke the words well, "Just as I said." Simon had his hand on the hilt of his dagger.

Isaiah took a deep breath and after a few attempts quieted the crowd enough to be heard once again. "Righteous men, with James' statement of support for the Essene way and the obvious unity we have shown tonight, I have no doubt that we can come to a well thought through answer to this threat that Jesus has given us."

He paused giving the impression that he was thinking through the proper way to proceed. In reality, James thought, the procedure had already been decided long before the meeting began.

"The Passover is tomorrow. We all have homes and family to prepare for the remembrance of our salvation from slavery. Let us adjourn for the Passover and assemble again on the sixth day in the afternoon before the Sabbath. That will give the Elders time to think through the appropriate response of Netzereth to Jesus' 'Triumphant Entry' into Jerusalem." Isaiah punctuated the last words with a mock bow. This again sent laughter through the assembly.

James had already motioned for his brothers to head for the door and they were out by the time the laughter died down.

"Speak to no one on your way home tonight. We will discuss this in the morning."

"We need to discuss this tonight brother." Judas replied with intensity on his face that rattled James.

"You may discuss this among yourselves but no where else. I need to get alone and think through some things. Tell Hadassah not to wait up for me." James immediately turned and walked away from his brothers.

James wandered the streets of Netzereth deep in thought. He stayed in the empty alleys of the newer sections of the village in order to be alone.

"Monster, heretic, abandoned the faith", the words from the assembly confirmed what he already knew to be true concerning the feelings of most people in Netzereth. And, in fact, the belief was his own view, but with less venom. But hearing the feelings voiced in such virulent ways renewed the turmoil of life that had been his reality for the past three to four years.

His thoughts turned to a discussion in an easier day. Jesus was on the roof of the homestead surveying the fields of the Esdraelon Plain and the Samaritan hills beyond. James often found his brother there. Usually he was in prayer or meditation at sunrise.

"The fields are ripe for harvest. The farmers will begin their long-awaited harvest this week. They prepared the ground, planted their seed, and weeded the land. Now it is time to begin the work they longed to enjoy six months ago." Jesus paused and James was going to remark about the family garden when Jesus began again. "It is almost time to begin the work I am here to do, James. I'm concerned about the impact my ministry will have on the family."

"When you sit on the throne of Israel, all the struggles to get there will seem insignificant. You know our whole family and all the Netzerim support your claim to the throne of David. We all know it will be difficult. The Romans aside, there are the struggles we will face convincing the Pharisees and Sadducees of your messiahship. The Pharisees control the thoughts and beliefs of a majority of Israel and the Sadducees control the Temple. And although both groups are corrupt we need their strength..."

"James, the path I take in the next year will be different than what you have been taught. There will be a time when even you will desert me and the work I do in the name of the Father of lights. But James," Jesus turned toward James and their eyes locked, "I need you to hold the family together. Promise me. The family will soon be your responsibility and you must protect them from internal strife. You have the strength to hold them together. Judas is headstrong, Joseph is fearful of authority figures and thus submits without thinking, and Simon is often angry and impulsive. The next few years are going to be very hard for all of you! Even when you turn against me, you must be strong for our family."

James objected, "Never, I will never turn against you. You are my big brother and the hope of our nation. Nothing will change between us."

Jesus smiled and turned his attention back to the fields. "I love you James. It is that very rejection of my words that will help you keep the family together despite the words of all those who speak against me." He paused, and then quietly added "Promise me please."

"A man who aimlessly walks the streets in the dark is generally working through a guilty conscience." The voice of Matthan abruptly brought James back to the present. Where had he come from? Had he been following since the meeting?

"A man who hides in the shadows and watches others may also be guilty of sin." James shot back.

"It is not me you should be worried about James. Everyone at the assembly heard what you had to say and saw the reactions of your brothers to the news of your demonic brother! Sure Isaiah put a positive spin on it but I know you do not fully support the Netzerim or our belief that Jesus is a false prophet."

"Take care in the words you use Matthan. I know you are new to Netzereth but there are many in this town that view my brother as the rightful heir to David's throne, verified by his lineage, birth, and angelic announcement!"

"All lies, and you know it. Your mother and father made up those stories of angel visits for their own corrupt ends and to hide their promiscuity or worse her prostitution. And we are all descendants of David here in Netzereth. We all claim to be of the 'branch' of Jesse. Jesus is no one special."

James felt the blood rush to his face, the pounding of his heart roared in his ears. He leaned to within an inch of Matthan's face and his frame dwarfed the bookish build of the scribe. "If you doubt the righteousness of my parents and my family I challenge you to prove it in assembly. Until then you will keep your venom in your filthy mouth. I know your kind. You prey on others to build yourself up. You are a white-washed tomb. On the outside you show peace but inside you harbor death. Leave my family alone." James delivered each word with even staccato precision and a healthy dose of saliva.

Matthan's eyes grew wide and he took step back from James and in a weak voice responded, "If it is a trial you want..."

James jumped at Matthan and the scribe ran, losing his turban and not stopping to pick it up. James watched till he was out of sight in the dark streets. He slammed his hand against the stone wall near him and let out a guttural cry.

"That didn't improve your situation James." he said out loud, as he rubbed his stinging palm.

There was only one place to which he knew he could go when he felt this confused about Jesus and this sickening dilemma. He needed the counsel of a wise man and the understanding of a good friend. And there was one man who could meet that need.

He had heard from Emma earlier in the day that her husband Jacob was back from his trip to Caesarea where he had bought new cloth for their shop. James headed in the direction of Jacob's home hoping he would not cross paths with Matthan before getting there or for that matter be seen entering Jacob's home.

Jacob and Emma still believed in Jesus whole-heartedly. They occasionally would close up shop to follow Jesus as he taught along the shore of the Sea of Galilee. They had been at James' home on the day Jesus left Netzereth to find John near the Jordan River. John, an Essene of Levitical stock, and a second cousin had built a following after his training at the wilderness school near the Dead Sea and was baptizing for repentance at the Jordan River. Jacob gave Jesus a seamless tunic at that time and prayed a blessing of the Almighty over him. It had been a happy day for the family and Netzereth as well. Now, only Jacob and a few others in Netzereth believed in Jesus' claim as Messiah. James was not one of those wholehearted believers, but he knew Jacob and his wife Emma were true friends and he still trusted his counsel.

Jacob's home on Market Street contained a textile shop in the front with a small room used for measuring patrons who not only bought the cloth but also wished to take advantage of Jacob's excellent tailoring skills. The living area behind the shop consisted of one room and a small courtyard. A gentle shout from the shop entrance brought Emma to the door immediately.

"Oh James, I'm so glad to see you. Hadassah has been worried about you since you did not return home with your brothers after the meeting. Jacob is in the courtyard. Please go in and you two talk. I will let Hadassah know you are here and fine." She paused and searched his eyes. "You are fine?" James nodded. Emma smiled, grabbed a shawl to cover her head and entered the street allowing James to shut the shop door.

Going through the back of the shop, James saw Jacob sitting in the soft glow of a small fire. "James my friend, come sit with me. I heard from others about the assembly. You must be... well to be honest I am not sure how you are feeling. But you don't look good."

"I had a confrontation with Matthan."

Jacob rolled his eyes and nodded. James sat next to him by the warm fire and stared into it. Jacob waited for a long minute for James to speak.

"Jacob, is my brother a monster?"

Jacob looked at James and waited again.

"They called him a heretic, a monster, the son of a harlot, a false prophet, a demon." His blood began to boil again as he listed the words. "Yes, I understand that he has angered some and in this latest event, even caused trouble for our town. But those words do not describe the man I know." He paused and Jacob listened to the silence. "Did I ever tell you about the time he blessed Joshua? Joshua was seven days old and we brought him to the synagogue to name him and for the covenant of circumcision. Isaiah took him in his arms and pronounced the traditional blessing of the Covenantal Children of Israel. He then performed the ceremony and of course Joshua screamed. In fact, he screamed so loud that no one could hear the prayer Isaiah offered to the Holy One."

Jacob nodded and smiled with remembrance. "It was the loudest sermon ever heard in that room."

James chuckled. "Well, poor Joshua cried all the way home. There was nothing Hadassah or I could do to sooth him. Then Jesus came to our room and asked if he could bless his namesake. We placed the child in his hands and immediately Joshua stopped crying. My loving brother then prayed this;

'To the Father of all men,
To the One of unending love,
To the Creator of all life,
Be thanks for the voice of this little one.
Endow him with wisdom to speak to the hearts of men.
Inspire him with words of truth that bring life.
Renew in him the songs of Your praise.
And enable him to glorify You.

James wiped the tears from his eyes and asked, "Does that sound like a monster to you?"

Jacob placed his hand on James' shoulder and James realized that he had been emotionally shaking as he felt the steady hand of Jacob on him.. "Now let me tell you another story about a baby. A young woman of Davidic descent was engaged to be married to a man of the Essene sect, or as our fathers used to say, 'a righteous one'. But before they were joined in marriage the young woman was found to be with child."

James knew where the story was going. He had heard it thousands of times. But he did not stop Jacob.

"The righteous man had in mind to divorce the girl quietly so that she would have opportunity to leave Israel and give birth to the baby away from all relatives and let strangers raise the child. They both knew that if the community knew she was pregnant she could be stoned to death. She had sent word to him through a mutual friend that she had important news but he was cautious about meeting with her for fear of social reprisals. But he loved her so much and felt she deserved at least one chance to explain herself. He met her that night. And it changed everything."

"Jacob, I have heard this story since childhood. This does not help me sort out the issues at hand."

"I think it does, brother. You see, until your father met with your mother that night and had an angelic visit of his own, he believed the wicked stories that were starting to rise concerning your mother. But after she explained that she had been chosen to fulfill the prophecies concerning the Netzer, the Branch, the Messiah... that she was the virgin of Isaiah that would bring forth the Ruler, the Branch of Jesse... that he was the descendant of David to raise the next King... that the Shoot from the stump of Jesse was the Messiah we Netzerim have all awaited, only then did the devastating facts of an unwanted pregnancy become the glorious facts of a fulfilled promise. Soon the whole village of Netzereth was excited about the birth of the Netzer Messiah."

James quizzically stared at Jacob.

Jacob smiled wide at James and shook his big frame with a friendly hand. "The worst news can suddenly change to the greatest opportunity when looked at with all the information and with eyes of faith. James, you don't have all the information yet."

"But the whole village no longer believes he is the Netzer Messiah. He has offended them with his association with the Pharisees. He has ridiculed the beliefs of the elders breaking the laws of the Sabbath. He cavorts with prosti-tutes, tax-collectors, and even Gentiles. Does that sound like a Messiah?"

"They don't have all the information or the eyes of faith. You know that I am still a believer in your brother. There are things I have seen and heard that you would not believe James. He heals the sick. He loves those who are hurting and broken. He releases those who are in bondage. He teaches the truth of the Father. He brings hope to the weary soul and encourages those who truly want to know the Father. Doesn't that sound like a Messiah?"

James sat, unresponsive with his head bowed. Jacob threw a small stick on the fire and whispered, "They don't even have all the information concerning what happened at the 'triumphant entry' as Isaiah called it."

Recognizing Jacob's use of the phrase, James asked, "Were you at the assembly?"

Jacob snorted. "Are you kidding they never told me about it. I was not wanted at the assembly but I have my spies James."

"Who?"

"James, I am probably the most vocal of Jesus' supporters here in Netzereth but I am not the only one. I know today was hard for you. But I assure you, he is not a monster, a heretic, a false prophet, or…, what was it, a demon?" Shaking his head with a reassuring smile he added, "We just do not have all the information yet."

CHAPTER 3

(Thursday morning)

Although the whole family was home, silence soaked the air. Even Joshua sat quietly on the steps to the roof playing with a small insect, lost in his own world. Hadassah busied herself in the great room with little Sarah while the brothers sat around a small fire to take off the morning chill.

"I've heard that our brother did more than ride into Jerusalem in a royal procession. The next day, it is said, he entered the Temple court of the Gentiles and chased out the money changers and livestock merchants." Joseph smiled and shook his head as he fiddled with a piece of grass in his fingers.

"Why do you laugh brother? This is serious. Jesus has brought all the attention of the Romans and, if what you say is true, the Sadducees, down on our little clan of Netzerim."

"I laugh Judas, because that story reminds me of the brother I grew up with. I can see him on that foal, no doubt quoting the messianic passage from the prophet Zechariah. I read the prophecy when we came home last night. It speaks of the Almighty One removing all foreign invaders from Israel and the Messiah declaring peace. I would think we would be happy about Jesus finally doing what we all expected him to do since birth. And then cleaning up the Temple to punctuate the message! That is something all the Netzerim have wanted to do since the Sadducees bought the High Priestly office from the Romans."

"I would be happy; in fact, I would be dancing on tables right now, if Jesus hadn't cut every political cord he had as the rightful Davidic King. He angered the thousands of Essenes, who would have supported him, by joining the Pharisees and moving his home and center of activity to Capernaum. He then cut the cord to his new friends by constantly speaking out against their hypocrisy. He has never made any overtures to the Zealots who would have fought to the death for him if he had. And we all know how he feels about the Sadducees. He rides into Jerusalem with a mere twelve committed followers and a crowd of fickle sign seekers. His kingship is doomed before it starts. In fact, can we call it a kingship? He rides in, to the acclaim of the rabble and then disappears. Our brother, who is fond of making speeches, doesn't even announce his claim to the throne!"

"So Judas, you do believe he has the right to the throne?!" Joseph kidded.

"Bah! Wipe that silly grin off your face brother. I imagine you will still be grinning when the Roman army stands outside our gate?"

"No, it is the Gentiles, of all the groups you mentioned Judas, who might be excited about what our brother did."

Simon interjected. "He is constantly preaching acceptance of the dogs into the kingdom! It is for that very reason he was rejected by the Netzerim. So if Joseph is right that he still has a right to the throne of David, it may be the Gentiles who win it for him."

"You are mistaken Simon. The Romans ruthlessly smother all attempts to resurrect the Davidic line. And that is why we are at risk here in Netzereth." Then, turning to Joseph who was still smiling, Judas added, "Why are you still smiling? Haven't you been listening to what I have been saying?"

"I have reason to be happy. I have found true love. Even this news about our brother can't dampen my spirits. Are you jealous?"

"What? You don't mean that little girl Zerah?" Simon said with a push on Joseph's shoulder. "She has no form! She's a stick. You better hope her family is fattening her up for you."

Joseph made a fist and waved it at Simon and bantered, "I'll fatten you up, starting with your lip, if you mock her beauty again."

"I hope I don't get this hopeless when I find a wife." Judas said with a shake of his head. "James, you have been too quiet. What are you thinking?"

"I am wondering," James sighed, "why Jesus would do something so foolish in our eyes. I'm hoping that we do not understand fully what he has done. Is there a good reason he would draw the attention of the Roman leaders as well as the Jewish leaders at a time when he is so weak militarily and politically?"

"It makes no sense to me," Simon thoughtfully whispered. "If he had an army stationed in Jericho and this stunt was just to fulfill scripture perhaps it would make sense. But he has basically cut his own throat by doing this. The leaders in Jerusalem have only to bring him up on charges of treason to the governor and he is destined for the cross!"

"If only he had been more observant of the Law. The leaders in Jerusalem may have let this slide if he hadn't stirred up their anger by disobeying their authority and crossing them at every chance." In disgust James pushed himself up from his chair and looked to the sky to find an answer for Jesus' actions.

"You are right James, but he is not acting any differently than he did when he lived with us."

"What do you mean Joseph?" James turned and looked at his brother with a confused face. "He was always obedient to authority. I should know, as second born I was the one who was constantly getting in trouble and mother and father would always tell me to be 'more like Jesus'." James badly imitated his parents in his complaint.

"What I mean," Joseph smirked, "is that whenever he disobeyed authority he was able to get the authority to see it his way. Remember the time he was absent from the Sabbath assembly in which he was to give the reading from the Torah? After the meeting, Isaiah and father searched for two hours for him."

"I remember," Simon interjected, "they found him at Widow Miriam's home eating with her and teaching her out of scripture."

Joseph continued, "That's right! He had disobeyed the wishes of his elders but he talked his way out of the trouble."

"What he did, brothers, was to show from scriptures that true religion is to look after widows in their distress and then he demonstrated that Widow Miriam being blind was in greater need of a Torah reading than all the sighted men of the assembly."

"Exactly James! That is what I am saying! He always was able to talk his way out of his disobedience. Remember the time he stayed behind in Jerusalem as a child? I was only nine years old but I remember vividly how upset our parents were and how they finally found him in the Temple. He didn't get the rod for that one either! So his crossing of the Sadducees and Pharisees at this time of his life shouldn't surprise us now." Joseph chuckled. "I miss that rascal."

"That 'rascal' is going to be the death of us Joseph!" Judas snapped.

"I agree with Judas," Simon added. "Jesus not only crossed the leaders of the Jews but he has also alienated all the Essenes by his message of the Almighty's care for the Gentiles." Simon paused, pulled a small stick from the flame and quietly continued. "Unfortunately, the Roman authorities don't care about that message, so they will not hesitate to wipe out all who are connected to Jesus. Netzereth appears to stand in the way of Rome. And the last time I checked the

Roman army is bigger than the Netzereth army!" He waved the smoldering stick around in the air to indicate the whole of Netzereth, causing Joseph to duck the hot end. "I think we should seriously consider leaving Netzereth for a while."

"Where would we go? There is no place that would protect us." James asked quietly as he paced around his brothers and the fire.

Simon looked up at James and responded quickly, "I have heard that a small group of freedom fighters are stationed in Gamla of the Decapolis."

"I'm not sure even the Zealots of Gamla would accept our presence," James responded. "I am as concerned as you two, Judas and Simon, but I don't think the Romans are our main concern. It seems to me that our own Netzerim brothers are our more pressing problem. Jesus has brought attention from the Romans to our small village but I fear it is what happens in the next few days here in Netzereth that will tear us apart. We need to commit to each other brothers. Judas you are our inside man. Your work as a scribe for Isaiah will help us stay current on the thinking of the elders. Can I count on you to stay true to family? And more importantly can I count on you to stay levelheaded?"

Judas nodded. James looked at the other two with an inquisitive stare and they also nodded. "Good! Tonight we celebrate Passover but I am sure the whole village is buzzing about last night's meeting. I want to know what they are saying. Judas, you will get our best information at the synagogue. Do you have reason to be there today?"

"I can continue my work on transcribing the prophets. That will put me in the scriptorium where I won't be seen but can hear everything in the assembly room."

"Great. Simon, do you have any deliveries to make today?"

"No but I can make the rounds and see if anyone wants to order any items."

"Good, keep your ears open. Find out what our neighbors are saying. Joseph and I will go to Market Street and ask around for thoughts from friends."

All four men stood and began to leave the courtyard when they were arrested by the shout from the great room.

"Where do you think you are all going?"

"We all have business to attend to."

"Your business is here husband. You promised to help me get the room ready for Passover meal. You also said you would spend time with Joshua so he would be ready to participate in his first Passover sacrifice! And the rest of you must clean your mess up. Simon and Joseph your tools are spilling out of the door of your room into the courtyard, again!"

"James, why does your wife think she is my mother?" Joseph jabbed at his brother in a whisper.

"Because if your mother were here she would tell you the same thing Joseph, and you know it." Hadassah responded as she walked by and slapped him on his chest..

All four men looked at each other in surprise. "She has the ears of a bat!" Judas said under his breath.

"Hadassah, Judas and Simon really do need to go do some work. But Joseph and I will stay to help you." James nodded to Judas and Simon to get going before she could respond. The two brothers quickly escaped out the courtyard gate and into the streets of Netzereth. "You really should clean up your tools Joseph." James put his arm around Joseph's shoulder and led him toward the room he was building for Zerah, his betrothed. "Here is another marriage lesson. The Almighty created male and female and their proper roles are that of leader and follower. But then He created marriage and when the two become one, the roles get confused a little."

"But she's not MY wife!"

"No, but she is mine and I am your older brother and head of household. So clean your room." They both smiled and got to work.

"How much cloth have we sold this week?" Jacob asked Emma when he joined her in their textile shop on Market Street.

"It wasn't a good week husband. I sold that black piece of Phoenician cloth on Sunday and that was it. I did get some small hemming jobs but that was it for the week. I don't expect there to be much business today because of Passover this evening."

"I saw Deborah this morning in a new head covering. It looked like the cloth I purchased last month in Caesarea. Didn't she buy it here?"

"No dear. She probably went to Cana to buy it. She has family there and her husband has told her not to buy from us anymore."

"Yes I remember her restriction. I just thought she might have come here when I saw the head covering. I was sure we had cloth like that here."

"We do." Her voice sounded excited but the meaning of the words was disappointing. "It's right here on the shelf." She pointed to the top shelf where they displayed all their best cloth.

"Well, we should probably expect business to get worse with the news of last night. I'm not sure how much longer we can continue to do business here in Netzereth. Jesus said we needed to count the cost of following Him. I guess our business and friends in Netzereth are also part of the cost." Jacob began to wonder how long they could continue to run a business in Netzereth and where else they could go to survive.

"We knew our friends here would be part of the cost but having the only textile shop in the village I thought would keep us going. I guess if they are willing to go to Cana or Nain or even Sepphoris then we will not be able to stay here much longer." Emma said seeming to read his mind.

"Sepphoris is the surprising one." Jacob shook his head as he continued, "Our Netzereth neighbors who despise the

Gentiles for being out of the grace of the Holy One and for corrupting our values and ruling over us, are willing to buy cloth from them in Sepphoris rather than us because we believe Jesus to be the promised Messiah!"

"Do not worry husband, this change of fortune for us is just a temporary trial." Emma smiled down at Jacob as he sat on a low stool with his head bowed. She stroked the back of his head and continued. "I was remembering this morning that picnic we had on the shore of Galilee."

At the word "picnic" Jacob raised his chin and grinned. It was their code word for the greatest event they had ever witnessed! "Yes we were all lucky you had packed that lunch for Jesse that morning."

"Well that is my point" Emma replied. "I think that even if Jesus didn't have the five small loaves of bread and two small fish, he could have fed the crowd. We need not worry about the downturn in our business, the Almighty can send manna."

Jacob felt his spirit reviving as he thought about it. "Amen and amen. There was so much left over that Jesus invited Jesse to refill his lunch pouch with three times as much bread and fish. Our momentary struggle is well worth the joy we have in knowing the Netzer of Israel, Jesus the Messiah."

Jacob stood and slapped the display counter of the shop. A remnant of cloth began to slide off the counter and Jacob grabbed it and folded it as he continued. "My dear, I think it is time for me to trust the Father with more than just my business. My friends, Jesus' family, need my voice. I must go to the assembly tomorrow morning and speak for Jesus and support James, Joseph, Judas, and Simon. If Jesus can feed over 5,000 people with five loaves and two fish, I can stand for him and pay the price of following him."

Emma smiled at him and nodded.

James and Joshua arrived at the home of Isaiah with the unleavened bread that Hadassah had made. James called out Isaiah's name and slapped the door frame twice.

"James, my son, welcome!" Isaiah unbarred the door and opened it wide.

"Hadassah sent us here with your bread for Passover. She wanted me to tell you that it is baked just as you like it with extra olive oil and herbs."

"Thank you James." Isaiah took the bread from his hand and placed it on a small stone ledge next to the door. "Please tell your woman she has blessed my home with her goodness. Do you have time to sit for a while with me?"

This is what James had hoped for and why he had brought Joshua along on the errand. James wanted more information on what Isaiah was thinking but he did not want a confrontation with Matthan. The presence of Joshua would keep everyone civil, he hoped.

Isaiah motioned to a bench just outside the door of his two-room home. The three of them sat, Joshua swung his feet and clucked his tongue. "James, I am so glad you spoke those words of support for the Netzerim cause last night."

"You know Rabbi, I care deeply for Netzereth and the Torah and the teachings of the Essenes. But I also have hope for my brother as well." Their eyes locked and James could tell that Isaiah was pleased with his words.

"That is admirable James, and I would not have expected anything less of you. However, it is clear to all of us that he is not the promised Branch whom Isaiah the prophet spoke of, nor the Prophet of whom Zechariah spoke." Isaiah looked intently into James' eyes and continued. "It would be very wise of you and your family to distance yourself from your brother at this time."

"What do you expect to happen tomorrow afternoon at the village assembly?" James asked, slightly lowering his head to demonstrate submission. He wanted Isaiah to feel comfortable enough with the conversation to let slip any real plans that had already been made.

"Well, that is yet to be seen. Perhaps it will just be a friendly discussion of the options open to us now that our little village has come to the attention of the Romans. Perhaps we will have to take some pre-emptive action to demonstrate to the heathens that we are innocent of any actions taken by Jesus of Netzereth. That is why it was important for you to speak up last night and demonstrate your support of the elders. I like you and your family, James. I will do all I can to help the leadership of Netzerim see your loyalty to them.

In any case, anyone who is not actively in support of your brother has nothing to fear."

Nothing to fear, James let the words roll around in his mind for a few seconds realizing that the real plan had been decided already. The secret followers of Jesus in Netzereth may not be as secret as they thought. And the obvious followers like Jacob and his family have been targeted.

"I would hope and pray that all those who call Netzereth home would have nothing to fear."

"I also pray for that my son. But unfortunately, we both know there are those who no longer follow the way of The Righteous. They have been blinded by smooth talking shepherds who only wish to fleece the sheep."

"Jesus is not the kind of person to fleece anyone." James rose from the bench, but Isaiah's thick hand pushed his thigh back down to the seat.

"James, please you must realize that the prophets warned us repeatedly that there would be false prophets who would come in the name of the Almighty. Your brother continues to claim that he is the Messiah and yet we know he is not. The obvious conclusion is that he is a false prophet. And those who continue to follow him will cause much pain and suffering for us in Netzereth. Jesus will be unsuccessful as the Messiah because the Almighty will bring him to his ruin, but his actions will bring Romans upon our small village in retribution long before Jesus is discovered to be the false prophet we know him to be."

Isaiah suddenly brightened as he caught the eye of Joshua who had been standing quietly a few feet away. "But we know the people of Netzereth will do the righteous thing in this matter, we are Essene after all aren't we Joshua?" Isaiah smiled, rose and gave Joshua's head a rub.

"Yes Rabbi." Joshua replied excitedly.

James couldn't argue with the logic of Isaiah, but he didn't like the path it led him down. He nodded a good-bye to Isaiah and was about to leave with Joshua when Matthan approached the house.

"Matthan, James and his boy just dropped off some wonderful unleavened bread for our celebration tonight! I have told you of the excellent baking that James' woman does. She is the best in the village. We will eat well tonight."

Matthan met James' eyes with a look of contempt that was hidden from Isaiah and said in a soft voice, "Thank you James."

"You are welcome Matthan. Isaiah is right my wife is the best bread baker in the village. So don't eat it too fast and choke on it." James smiled at Matthan and then turned to Joshua, "Come son, let's get home for our celebration."

Matthan watched the two walk away until they turned a corner and then went inside the house where Isaiah was busy organizing the bread amongst the other foods brought over by neighbors.

"We are tremendously blessed by the Almighty this Passover. Look at this fine food our disciples have supplied for us."

"He is no disciple of ours and you know it Isaiah."

"He is a good man, a Righteous man. He will make the right decision when he understands what is at stake."

"That's just it Isaiah, we coddle these heretics hoping they will see the truth of our teaching but they follow a charlatan, an imposter to the throne of David. They deserve to be put out of the Synagogue at least and are most likely deserving of death for their belief in this Jesus." Matthan spit the last few words out through clenched teeth.

"I warn you, Matthan. Be careful how you speak of the people in this village, and particularly James. Yes, Jesus is a heretical teacher. And we must do something about the many Essenes who still follow him blindly, especially in our clan of Netzerim. We know that the Messiah will come from us, the line of David, and this Jesus has capitalized on that so our work to turn his followers back to righteousness is especially difficult. But these are my friends and family, Matthan. I will support and protect them as a good shepherd. And we do not have definite proof that James is a follower of his brother. So I caution you, don't move too fast in attacking those who you think follow Jesus."

"Too fast? We don't have time to move slowly. The Romans do not take kindly to kingly announcements in the land they rule!"

"I realize that, but if you take the long view you will see that Jesus himself has hurt his following among the Netzerim far more than we could have by condemning his actions." Isaiah continued with a well rehearsed list of mistakes Jesus had made. "He refused to perform any signs of his authority when he was here. He cavorts with gentiles. He taught in our own synagogue that we were not worthy of the Almighty's attention. He moved to Capernaum and joined the heretic Pharisee sect. All of these events have lost followers among the Netzerim. Jesus is his own worst enemy."

"But Isaiah, we need to show the world that we are not in support of Jesus in any way. And what the Romans will understand is a total eradication of any followers of a usurper to the throne. They only understand blood. Will it be our blood or theirs?"

The veins were sticking out on Matthan's neck and Isaiah sat with a sigh on one of the stools next to the table loaded with food. "We may have to use some force and hand over the followers of Jesus to the Romans but I am convinced that James and His family are not part of that group. So you, Matthan, will follow my lead and we will protect our village. But we will not turn over innocent people as scapegoats for the Romans' bloodlust. Do you understand me?"

"Yes Rabbi, as you say." Matthan turned quickly and left the house.

"Mighty One of Israel, give me wisdom and patience with this young one." Isaiah sighed and went back to arranging the table for the Passover meal.

CHAPTER 4

(Thursday Afternoon)

"You let him name the lamb?" James stared at Hadassah with the knife in half stroke on the whet.

"I didn't let him. He just did it. James, we have sent him down to the stable three times a day the past week to check on the Passover Lamb to make sure it has not been hurt in any way. It was inevitable that he would fall in love with it and give it a name."

"And now I have to take him down to the stable to kill his pet?"

Hadassah smiled and held James' left forearm and leaned her head against his shoulder. Her touch relaxed his muscles and thoughts. She lifted her eyes to look into his and said, "You know, my brothers and I had the same issues when we were young. My father once told us that the reason the Almighty chose a year-old lamb as the Passover meal was because they are so cute."

James ran his finger along her jaw line and lovingly pinched her chin. "Your father always was a little strange in his thinking about the ways of the One." James looked up into the cloudless sky and sighed. "So why did he say that? Maybe I can get some clever words to soften the blow for Joshua."

"That's just it." She replied with a smile. "The killing of the lamb is to be precious to us. When we killed the lamb in Egypt to escape the hand of Pharaoh it was in substitution of the firstborn male of every household. We are not asked to kill unhealthy lambs, we are asked to spill the blood of perfect, cute little lambs, lambs we value, because the people for whom they substitute are valuable."

James stood silently. Her description of her father's teaching about the Passover lamb brought back some memories of his own.

"What are you thinking?" she asked.

James turned back to the table and began sharpening the knife again before speaking. "I was thinking of the year when Jesus named the Passover Lamb. We were older than Joshua is now but we were still young. I was about eight, I guess. So, Jesus was ten. That year he told me that he had named the lamb. It was the only time I remember us doing that. He named it Zelophehad."

"That's a strange name for a lamb."

"It was the name of the father in the wilderness wanderings who had only daughters and no sons to inherit land when the nation entered the Promised Land." James stopped sharpening the knife and carefully ran the blade across his palm. "I asked him why he named the lamb that, and he said it was because the name meant 'first-born' and the lamb was to be a substitute for the first-born in the family. When I mentioned it to my father he told me that the name also means 'shadow from terror' and was a reminder of that night when the Egyptians loss their first-born sons and Israel was saved."

Hadassah gently took the knife from James and placed it on the nearby table, "Can we talk about him please?"

James sighed, looked up, and then closed his eyes. When he lowered his head he looked straight into Hadassah's eyes. "Hadassah when he left Netzereth and moved his base of teaching to Capernaum, he abandoned our way of thinking. He embraced the Pharisees. He no longer wished to listen to reason. We went to him and asked him to come back home. He wouldn't come back. Don't you remember? He left and placed me in charge of the family. I love my crazy brother, but he has sown his own seeds and it looks like they are about to sprout. Unfortunately the fruit is falling on Netzereth and our family as well."

"Yes I remember you and your brothers going to see him and I also remember that it was after that trip that your mother began following Jesus regularly. Isn't it possible that she found something in his words to believe?" Hadassah pleaded for a positive answer with her eyes.

"He always had wonderful words to say, but he also had difficult words to hear. When we went to bring him back to Netzereth he said that only his disciples were his family. I know what he meant, but what he said hurt. It is as if he had turned his back on his heritage and his family and such a thing should never be done."

"But James the truth is that your mother heard those words as well and believed. Were not his exact words, 'whoever does the will of my Father in heaven is my brother and sister and mother'?" Hadassah untied the whet from the table and sat down on one of the benches. She turned the whet over in her hands looking at it carefully before continuing. "Is it possible that the way of the Netzerim is not the way of the Messiah?"

"How can you say that woman?" James sat down opposite her. "You know that the Netzerim are the direct descendants of David. You know that the prophecies tell us that the Messiah would be born in the line of David. The Netzerim have waited faithfully for the One to act and bring this deliverance through us. It is the way of the Netzerim that has made possible the deliverance through the Messiah."

"Really? I thought it was the Almighty that has made possible through the Netzerim the Messiah's salvation."

James tilted his head and gave Hadassah a look of impatient disbelief. "You know what I mean."

"Yes I do James. But do the Netzerim know what they mean?" James furrowed his brow in inquiry. "What I mean is, have the Netzerim become so full of themselves that they are no longer willing or able to hear the One's voice or do His will? Jesus may be calling the Netzerim back to their true role of obedience. And it may have hurt Jesus even more to say the words that hurt you knowing that the Netzerim, his own people, were not willing to hear and obey the Almighty."

James began to feel the ire arise inside him. "My brother has always pushed the boundary markers of polite conversation. I can think of only a few times when he didn't say things that put someone on the edge of his seat. Why does he have to be so controversial? It's his own fault if he feels badly about what he says. He could have done much more to endear himself to the people of Israel." James stood suddenly and took three paces away from the table, deep in thought.

Hadassah stood and moved to his side, placing a hand on his shoulder. "You are probably right James. But whenever I had opportunity to speak with him he indicated that his goal was not to please other men but rather please the Almighty. And isn't that the kind of messiah we would hope for?"

"Hadassah! You sound like Jacob and Emma." James took Hadassah by both shoulders and looked her squarely in the eyes. "You are not a follower of Jesus. You can not be. It is too dangerous! As the head of this house, I forbid it!"

"Yes my husband, as you say." Hadassah turned away and went into the great room of the homestead.

James mentally kicked himself as he watched her go. Why had he been so harsh with his words? She was right, but the kind of right that could leave someone dead. Didn't she understand the danger in saying such things? Although he had not treated her any different than any other man would have treated his wife, James had built a different marriage than others. And he knew Jesus had taught him to love his wife. Jesus had really chosen a pearl for him by arranging a marriage with Hadassah. She was a hard worker, she respected him as a man, she was an excellent mother, and although her deformity had turned away other suitors, it had made her a compassionate person for those who needed love. She was lovely in form and substance. She was also one of the most insightful people he knew. That was why he enjoyed talking with her and kept her by his side while walking in public rather than making her follow like a servant as other men made their women do. He loved her. And he had just dismissed her thoughts because of his own insecurity, and fear for her safety.

He turned to go to her and apologize but there was Joshua walking towards him.

"Eema said you needed to see me abba." Joshua's large brown eyes looked up at him. James sighed and looked beyond Joshua to the door of the great room where Hadassah was standing. There was a slight smile on her face and a tear on her cheek as she mouthed "It's okay." and blew him a kiss.

James knew he had a pearl of great price. He mouthed, "Thank you." And then he turned his gaze back to Joshua. "My son, your mother tells me that you named the Passover lamb?"

"Yes father. His name is fluffy! Are we going to go see him now?"

"Yes we are. And on the way to the stable I am going to tell you about the time your uncle Jesus named the Passover lamb." James grabbed the knife off the table, laid his hand on the back of Joshua and led him to the garden gate.

Three hours later the Passover lamb was roasting, Joshua had dried his tears, and the brothers were sitting around the cooking fire tending the meat and discussing the only topic of any importance in Netzereth. Joseph had cleaned up the mess outside the room he was preparing for Zerah and himself. Simon had spent the day roaming the marketplace and visiting former customers. He had generated a bit of business which he planned to start after Shabbat, but more importantly he had heard some more news about how Netzereth was reacting to the "triumphant entry" of Jesus into Jerusalem. Judas heard very little at the synagogue. A few elders of the village had come by but they were more concerned about getting their homes ready for Passover.

"The majority of the people I spoke with were not so much concerned with the actions of Jesus as much as they were with the fall-out it would bring on them personally." Simon shifted his weight on the stool and leaned in closer to his brothers who were around him. "They have lived in constant fear, a shadow of dread covers every part of their life and now the shadow is deepening!"

"But if I am hearing you correctly they really don't have a hatred of Jesus as much as a fear of the Roman threat, correct?" James asked.

"That's right. Of course, there are some who hate our brother because of the fear they have. It is easier to put all your frustration on someone who is not here than to take responsibility yourself for the world around you. But many people remember with fondness our brother who just a short time ago lived in this home and helped build their homes."

"I was remembering our last Passover with Jesus." Joseph stood up and walked to the table and poured himself a cup of wine. "He always made the history of our people so interesting. He explained the story of the ten plagues and our escape as if he had actually been there!"

"I agree," added Judas. "It was his stories that encouraged me to become a scribe. I wanted to spend my time immersed in the things that he found so interesting." After a long pause in which all four men stared into the flames, he added, "Funny how things can change so quickly."

There was a feminine call at the gate. Simon jumped up to answer the call. "That must be the servant girls with the water." When he opened the gate two women entered with large water jugs on their heads. They walked across the courtyard and proceeded to pour the water from their jars into the larger holding jar near the door of the great room.

"There is another thing that has changed." Joseph smiled, "Remember when Jesus would be the one to fetch the daily water from the town well? I used to be so embarrassed to see my oldest brother doing woman's work."

Simon paid the women at the courtyard gate and returned to the fire. "I'm still embarrassed about that. Our sisters were certainly capable of fetching water for the family and I know they often did until they married and moved away, but Jesus always insisted on helping them. It was beneath his stature as head of the household."

"I always appreciated that about him." The words came from Hadassah who had approached the brothers from her room where she had just laid Sarah down for a quick nap. "When I was pregnant with Joshua, he insisted on doing the water fetching all the time. I knew he was busy with his own work but he always was willing and available to be a servant to the family. He knew that others were talking about him and his obvious reversal of roles but he didn't care. He led this family by serving."

"So, with Jesus in Jerusalem, it falls to you again brother, to lead us in the Passover meal. Are you ready to wow us like you did last year?" The irony in Judas' voice caused Joseph and Simon to snicker.

"What I know is that little Joshua will do a much better job than Simon did last year in asking the teaching questions." James gave Simon a playful shove on the shoulder. He then turned to Hadassah and said, "The lamb is almost ready. Is everything else ready?"

"Final details like getting these chairs into the great room and lighting the candles are all we still need to do. So as soon as you pronounce the end of the day I will wake Sarah and we can begin the celebration."

"The ram's horn will sound at dusk to mark the end of the day and the beginning of Passover. I had to listen to Saul

Ben Daniel practice on the horn for over 40 minutes this afternoon in the synagogue. This is his first High Holy Day sounding and he wants to make sure the whole village can hear it." Judas rubbed his ears and shook his head as he stood up. "Come on men lets get these chairs to the table, the smell of the lamb is making me extremely hungry, and I want to be ready to eat as soon as possible."

CHAPTER 5

Isaiah stood as the ram's horn signaled the end of the fifth day and the beginning of Passover. "Blessed are You Almighty, Maker of heaven and earth. You brought Israel out of bondage by Your mighty hand. You led them through the wilderness to make them truly Your own people. You gave them Your law through the prophet Moses and taught them to obey with mighty acts of devastating power. You went before them into the Promised Land, a land of great delights and You drove out the sinful nations so that Israel could live in peace and worship You. It is because of Your work for us that we remember these events with this meal and look forward to Your Messiah's coming to once again deliver us from bondage under the godless heathens that occupy the land You gave to Israel."

Standing around the table as Isaiah gave the opening blessing of Passover were four other men. To Isaiah's right was Matthan. He was given the seat of honor next to Isaiah because his apprenticeship was almost over and he would soon be given the role of lead rabbi in the village. To the right of Matthan was Heber, a friend of Matthan who also went to the wilderness school but could not perform to the high standards that the Qumran rabbis required and was sent home to Netzereth to learn a secular trade. Next to Heber was Nathaniel. Nathaniel had been invited to share in Isaiah's celebration of Passover because his whole family had been killed by the Romans in the past five years. His father died at the hands of a drunken soldier. His mother and sister were taken away as slaves to pay back taxes. They both died in captivity, his sister while giving birth to a child fathered by her Roman master. He was alone, bitter and existing only to bring vengeance on the oppressors from Rome.

Finally, to the left of Isaiah was the head Elder in Netzereth, Jeremiah. He was there primarily for the same reason all the others were, he was single, a widower. Each one of these men was part of "the leftovers" club, as they jokingly referred to themselves. None of them had any family with whom to eat holy meals. The Leftovers often came together for such events and became a family of their own.

"All praise to the Almighty who has blessed us with His bountiful hand and has chosen us, the Righteous Ones, to be the Netzer from which the Messiah will come to save all of Israel." Although Matthan prayed this in Aramaic, he used the Hebrew word for "shoot" for two reasons. Mainly he wished to impress the others with his knowledge of Scripture by means of a conversation about the Isaiah promise that a shoot from the stump of Jesse would rise to be a kingly messiah. And also he wanted to begin to explore the options they had to removing the Jesus threat on Netzereth.

"Amen." All five men chorused together and then reclined at their places around the table.

As head of the group, Isaiah picked up the pitcher of wine and poured a cup for himself indicating the beginning of the meal. Matthan's blessing ploy worked as Elder Jeremiah was the first to speak.

"The Netzer will assuredly be a descendant of our tribe, Matthan, but how will we recognize him? Many have come in the last century who claimed to be the one but they have all proven to be impostors."

"The prophet tells us, Elder Jeremiah, that the Netzer will be anointed with the spirit of the Almighty and judge in favor of the poor and needy bringing judgment on the wicked Gentiles by slaying them with His very words. His work will gather all the exiles of Israel to him here in this land and cause all foreign nations to bow before his might."

"That is a completely different picture than what I have seen of this latest pretender." Heber interjected. "Jesus of Netzereth coddles the gentile scum that come to him. He is definitely not the Netzer."

"But there are many in this very village," Nathaniel murmured as he bit into a handful of lamb, "who would say that he is the Netzer."

"And they are tragically wrong." Matthan responded defiantly. "It is tragic that some of those who have been deceived by Jesus must suffer the consequences of their sin so that the truth may prevail."

"And what do you suggest are the consequences? Because we must not forget, my young apprentice, that as the leaders of the Netzerim, we are commissioned to protect even those who are mistaken about the identity of the Messiah as we teach them the truth."

"But Master, isn't it true that sometimes a portion of the flock must be sacrificed for the good of the whole flock? In a land where there is little water and food to graze upon, the good shepherd will slaughter the weak sheep so that there will be enough for the others. I believe we live in a time of little resources. This Jesus has sapped the faith of some of the Netzerim and created a spiritual waste land here in the very heart of true Israelite faith. We must, as good shepherds, do something that will turn the hearts of the people back to their Creator and prepare the way for the true Netzer to come." Matthan hoped that he had not come across too strong and had ended his statement with a plaintive tone.

Both Heber and Nathaniel nodded their agreement. Isaiah thoughtfully moved his food around on his plate and sighed.

Jeremiah swallowed and asked, "Who are the wicked that the prophet Isaiah speaks of?"

"Isaiah speaks of Judah and Ephraim swooping down upon the slopes of Philistia and plundering Edom, Moab, and Ammon. The primary enemies are the heathen gentiles." Matthan paused, smiled, and continued while dangling a piece of bread just inches from his mouth. "Of course there is the indication that the judgment of the Messiah for the poor and needy is against not only the foreign oppressor but also the unrighteous among us. And what is more unrighteous than believing in a false messiah and leading others to destruction as well?"

"I would not mind helping the Messiah rid us of the heathen among us. Do we have to wait for the Netzer to arrive to begin driving these Romans from our land?"

"Nathaniel, I know your heart is hurting because of the loss of your family but beware lest you become too anxious in your desire for justice. We must await the coming of the true Netzer and join His cause on our behalf." Isaiah stood and went to the door of his home. "Please excuse me my friends. I am not feeling well. I will return shortly."

The remaining group of men listened as Isaiah rounded the outside of his home and went to his room at the back of the house.

Heber spoke first. "So I would think that it would be a great service to the true Netzer to get rid of the false one and those who follow him."

"I agree brother, I would also like to be rid of the unsavory elements of our village, but as an elder of Netzereth I must insist that any action we take be with the approval of Isaiah. He is our leader. We must be prudent in our plans to rid the followers of Jesus from our midst."

Matthan had been hoping this conversation could happen today and took advantage of the opportunity. "I agree Jeremiah. So let's start thinking through what we can do and what obstacles are in our way so that the unrighteous among us can be eliminated." He paused and then added, "And it is only right that those who plow the field take part in the harvest, yes?"

All four men smiled at the thoughts that Matthan's words brought to mind. They were about to become the saviors of the truly righteous and enjoy some personal gain in the process.

James stood as the ram's horn signaled the end of the fifth day and the beginning of Passover. "Blessed are You Almighty, Maker of heaven and earth. Unto You all glory and praise for You have shown yourself to Your people as holy, faithful, and merciful. You have brought us to this promised land by Your mighty hand and have sustained us by Your power. We are your chosen people to bring Your Name to the Nations. We are Your chosen people to bring Your Messiah to the nation. We are Your chosen people to proclaim Your praise to the world. Bless this remembrance of Your Passover by coming to Your people in power. All praise to the Almighty who has blessed us with His bountiful hand and has chosen us, the Righteous Ones, to be the Branch from which the Messiah will come to save all of Israel."

All the men at the table said "Amen" in unison with Joshua just a beat behind the adults.

"Thank you, Hadassah for working so hard to prepare this wonderful meal. The roasted lamb smells delicious, the unleavened bread looks like golden discs of sweetness, and the fruit is mouth watering." James then looked at Joshua and asked, "What do you think son?"

"Why do we eat bitter herbs?" He responded hesitantly.

Everyone chuckled, and Judas corrected Joshua, "You are a little early with the questions Joshua. I think your father wanted you to say thank you to your mother for all her hard work." He tussled the boy's hair and turned to Hadassah. "I must admit, woman, this is one of the finest Passover meals I have ever seen. Thank you."

"Yes thank you." Both Simon and Joseph affirmed. Joseph did so with a mouth full of bread which he was obviously enjoying.

"You are all very welcome but I am sure this does not compare to the meals your own mother prepared in the past."

All four men stopped eating and looked at each other. "Hadassah, you have eaten our mother's cooking. Surely you know the joy we all experienced when James married you and brought you to live here with us." Judas continued. "We love our mother. She is a spiritual rock. She loves us with an undying love. And she always knew how to challenge us to do our best, but her one weakness was at the cooking fire."

"And she knew it as well." James chimed in. "I remember one Passover she convinced father to hire other women of the village to prepare most of the meal."

"I remember that as well but I thought it was because she was about to give birth to our youngest sister." Joseph reached for more fruit. "But that was a good meal." And he punctuated the statement by tossing a fig in the air and catching it in his mouth.

"I think that was the main reason we usually traveled to Jerusalem for Passover." Simon added. "Some of our relatives in the Righteous community up there really knew how to cook."

"How often did your family travel to Jerusalem? I remember my family made the required trip maybe twice during my childhood."

James broke some bread and dipped it in the salt water which was meant for the bitter herbs. It was an idiosyncrasy of James that he loved that dip which was supposed to remind them of the bitter tears of Egypt. "We probably traveled to Jerusalem around ten to thirteen times in my first 27 years. We tried to go every other year. Our parents believed it was important that our first year as full adults in the community be celebrated at Passover in Jerusalem."

"Do you remember how every trip Mother would make us count off in the morning as we woke?" Simon nudged Joseph with his elbow. "You hated that didn't you?"

"It was such an obvious ploy to get us to start talking to them early in the morning. It was a reaction to the year that

Jesus disappeared without letting them know where he was going." Joseph pointed his finger at James and shook it to punctuate each word. "Don't do that to your children."

"Actually, I kind of like the tradition, Jesus and I sort of had fun with it counting off in different languages. And as a parent I appreciate the goal of the exercise. I assure you, none of you worried our parents in the same way Jesus did on that one trip."

"I don't know this story," Hadassah interjected. "What happened?"

"On the day we were to leave Jerusalem and return to Netzereth, Jesus went to the Temple area to discuss a new idea he had come up with from his nightly reading of the Torah. Our parents thought he was with Tobias' family helping them pack up for the return trip. When the whole troop was ready to head out they just assumed He was still with the group. We traveled two days before realizing he was not with us." James paused and took another bite of lamb.

"Two days?" Hadassah asked in shock. "Why didn't they get worried earlier? I would be frantic if Joshua was missing from my sight for two minutes much less two days."

"This event happened after his twelfth birthday so he was nearly an adult already and you need to think of Jesus slightly different than other people. He matured so fast. Most people thought he was thirteen at age nine" Joseph added.

"So what happened next?" Hadassah asked.

James swallowed and continued, "Well, our parents handed us off to some friends to continue the trip home and they went back to Jerusalem to look for Jesus. After searching the "Righteous Ones" community they finally found him at the Temple talking to the teachers of the law. They were embroiled in some discussion of the importance of the tense of a particular verb."

"It is a very important point that he was making," Judas passionately interjected. "He was proving the reality of the afterlife by referring to how the Almighty is the God of the living and is often referred to as the God of Abraham long after Abraham's death. It's an important truth that the Sadducees miss."

Everyone stopped eating for a moment and starred at Judas.

"Well, it is." Judas yelled with mock offense.

After a short pause and snicker, James continued, "Anyway, they found Jesus in the Temple and, as it was told to me later by Jesus, our father was quite upset with him." James then did a respectable imitation of his father. "Son, as an adult you should make wiser choices in how you conduct yourself. Why were you not concerned with the business of the family as we were preparing to leave and travel back to Netzereth?"

"Hey, not bad brother, but his voice was a bit deeper." Joseph said in a spot-on imitation of his father.

All the men had a good laugh and James continued. "Mother, in her softer approach said, 'Son, why have you treated us like this? Your father and I have been anxiously searching for you.' And Jesus asked them why they had to search for him they should have known where to find him. He was doing family business in his Father's house."

The three brothers chuckled at Jesus' answer but Hadassah and James locked eyes over the table as an unspoken, familiar, discussion was exchanged between them concerning Jesus' role as the Branch.

They were interrupted by the voice of their son Joshua. "Is it time abba?"

"Hmm? Time for what?"

"Is it time to ask? Joshua looked up at James' eyes with eager expectation.

"Yes it is time." James responded with a smile.

"Why is this night different?"

James looked at his son to emphasize the teaching. "Tonight is different because it represents our change from slaves of the world to children of the Most Holy. This night was our rebirth as a nation fully committed to obey and follow the Almighty. We must never forget who we were, how the Almighty saved us, and who we are now. What in particular do you see that is different tonight?"

"Why is this bread different?"

"We eat unleavened bread tonight to remember the haste in which our forefathers left Egypt. There was no time to allow the bread to rise. They ate with their sandals on and their walking staff nearby. They were about to be rescued from the hand of Pharaoh as the angel of the Almighty passed over every home in Egypt to destroy the firstborn of every home that did not have the blood of the covenant on their doorposts. The unleavened bread also reminds us of the purity that the Almighty requires as leaven represents sin, also a perfect lamb was slain to provide the blood of the covenant."

James picked up a piece of the unleavened bread and broke it in two. "Blessed art Thou, Giver of our daily bread." He passed the bread around the table and everyone took a portion for their plate.

James then reached for the parsley and saltwater dip. He dipped the parsley twice in the bowl and held it before him. "Blessed art Thou, Holy One, who has made us His own."

"Why do we eat bitter herbs?" Joshua looked at his mother with pride as he had remembered the words that had stymied him so much in practice with her.

Hadassah gave him a smile and head nod in approval.

"We eat bitter herbs to remind us of the pain and sorrow we had in Egypt before our deliverance. The salt water is our tears of agony as we worked to build the kingdom of Egypt and worked in Pharaoh's fields."

Joshua took some parsley and dipped it twice in the salt water. "Why do we dip the sour, um bitter herbs twice?"

James stifled a smirk. "We dip the herbs twice to remember the sorrow of the rebellion of our forefathers in the desert at Kadesh. It was there that they refused to enter the land which the Almighty had given to them. They refused to remember the mighty hand of the Holy One who delivered them from Egypt and were punished with forty years of desert dwelling. The first dip is for the sorrow of

Egypt and the second dip is the sorrow of disobedience in the desert."

James then pulled a piece of mutton from the bones in the center of the table. "Blessed art Thou, Deliverer, Thou hast provided a perfect sacrifice and blood of the Passover to protect and save us from our bondage."

"Why are we eating roasted lamb?" The words came softly from Joshua, and James remembered the struggle they had endured in the slaughtering of 'Fluffy'.

"We are eating roasted lamb, my son, because the Almighty requires a complete sacrifice. When we are finished with our meal we will burn the rest of the lamb in the fire because it all belongs to Him. The Holy One is not pleased with a partial sacrifice or a half-hearted devotion to Him. He deserves all of us, all our will, all our strength all our intellect, all of our heart. The roasted lamb reminds us to be totally devoted to Him. And the Almighty blesses us with His bounty which we partake in by eating the meat of the lamb."

James stood from the table and walked to where his son was sitting, knelt behind him and hugged him. He whispered in Joshua's ear, "Do you understand my son?"

Joshua nodded.

Jacob stood as the ram's horn signaled the end of the fifth day and the beginning of Passover. "Blessed are You

Almighty, Maker of heaven and earth. Unto You all glory and praise for You have shown Yourself to Your people as holy, faithful, and merciful. You have brought us to this promised land by Your mighty hand and have sustained us by Your power. We are Your chosen people to bring Your Name to the nations. We are Your chosen people to bring Your Messiah, Jesus, to the nation. We are Your chosen people to proclaim Your praise to the world. Bless this remembrance of Your Passover by coming to Your people in power. All praise to the Almighty who has blessed us with His bountiful hand and has chosen us, the Righteous Ones, to be the Branch from which the Messiah has come to save all of Israel."

Jesse and Emma joined Jacob in the "Amen."

"You have prepared an excellent meal for us again this Passover, woman!"

"And you and Jesse have roasted the lamb to perfection, husband. I was thinking earlier of the words of Jesus at the picnic last year. He said something like, 'the kingdom of heaven is like leaven which leavened three measures of flour.' I have spent a whole week removing all leaven from our home because it represents sin. How can Jesus say that the kingdom of heaven is leaven?"

"That is an interesting question. I remember that statement was said in one of his stories that he seldom explains. Some of his stories I get, but some are beyond my understanding."

"Father," Jesse interrupted, "is leaven really sin? The teaching at Passover is that we eat unleavened bread to remind us that our ancestors did not have time to wait for the bread to rise and had to be ready to go when Pharaoh released them after the angel of the Lord passed over their homes. What does that have to do with sin? And if leaven is sin why do we eat it at other times?

"Now wait a minute!" Jacob feigned agitation. "These are not the prescribed questions for Passover meal." He smiled and patted their hands on either side of him. "But let's see if we can think this through. You are right Jesse; leaven is not sin. It represents sin in the events of Passover because it symbolizes disobedience in being ready to leave Egypt at a moment's notice. That is also why we eat a whole roasted lamb rather than butcher it properly and remove the bones. Leaven and a butchered lamb would have been disobedient to the Almighty's instructions to be ready for a new way of life with Him." Jacob caught Emma's eyes and pointed to the lamb and herbs on the table.

"That still doesn't solve the kingdom of heaven and leaven teaching of Jesus." Emma said as she passed the platter of food to her husband.

"I think it starts us down the right path. Leaven is not sin. But it represents sin sometimes. So maybe it represents something else with Jesus' teaching. It represented sin because it caused people to hesitate as it works instead of being ready for the Almighty's action. What else does leaven do?"

"It causes dough to rise." Jesse almost shouted as he began to get excited about the mental treasure hunt his father had started.

"It changes the bread." Emma added. "And it permeates the whole lump of dough."

"Interesting, and so, would you two say that it is very powerful in its own way?" They nodded as they ate. "So maybe the Kingdom of Heaven will permeate and change everything it touches and bring real change, perhaps a rise in spiritual understanding and obedience. That is what I am hoping for Jesus to do when he becomes king." Jacob took a big bite of lamb, smiled, and sat back in his chair, pleased with himself.

Emma and Jesse looked at him and waited for further insight. He took another bite of lamb before noticing that they were staring at him.

"Don't you understand? Jesus is the Messiah. He has come to set up the kingdom of heaven here in Israel. And when he finally takes the throne of David he will change everything with the power of the Almighty."

"But" Emma questioned, "if he wanted to be king, couldn't he have had the position last year? After the picnic all the people, over 5,000 of them, wanted to make him king when they saw what he did with Jesse's lunch. I think he made it clear that he did not want to start a kingdom yet on this world."

"Of course he wants to be our king. That is why he was born. All the prophecies point to his ascension to David's throne." Jacob had spoken forcefully but then paused in thought and before continuing. "But you are right he did shy away from the up swell of adulation that afternoon." Jacob paused and then added with a snort, "He acted more like a lamb than the lion of Judah."

"The Passover lamb." Jesse quipped.

Jacob and Emma looked at each other and then at Jesse and then back at each other. They were both lost in thought for a minute until Jesse who was becoming concerned with the silence said again, "the Passover lamb?"

"You know he may have something there." Jacob turned the thought over in his mind a while before speaking again. "The Passover lamb is sacrificed and its blood put on the door frames of our homes to save us from the angel of death. Its life is given in place of the first born and it is a symbol of God's care for the nation of Israel."

"More than that, husband, its sacrifice created a new era of Israel's dealings with the Almighty. We became a nation. We became the people with whom The One resides. Our lives were changed in a remarkable way. We were slaves; we became children of the Almighty."

"But father, the Passover lamb dies." Jesse's words were filled with fear and doubt at the same time.

"OH." Emma gasped. "What did Philip say about how John the Baptizer introduced Jesus to him? Wasn't it, 'Behold the lamb of God who takes away the sin of the world.'?" Tears welled up in her eyes as she looked at Jacob.

Jacob knew she was hoping he would tell her she was wrong. But Jacob could not think of a way to console her. Instead, what came to mind was a memory from the many times he had listened to Joseph and Mary tell of their remarkable encounter with angels.

"And do you remember what the angel told Joseph in a dream? He was to call the child Jesus because he would save his people from their sin. How would a king save us from our sin?"

"A king would save his people from invading armies." Jesse said.

"It looks like we may have been looking for Jesus to be a king because of our national need and the excitement we would feel of having him come from Netzereth."

"I think you have a good thought there, Emma. Have we been trying to force Jesus into our idea of a king when in actuality He came to be a lamb… a Passover lamb to shed his blood and cover us from the wrath of God on sin?"

"Husband, this changes everything." Emma declared. "It means that Jesus isn't trying to set up a kingdom here. Instead, he is trying to sacrifice himself. And all the fears that the elders of Netzereth have concerning his display at Jerusalem this week are meaningless. Jesus will not bring the Romans down on us. He isn't interested in being our king. He wants to be our… Lamb."

CHAPTER 6

Jacob, Emma, and Jesse were up with the sun to get ready for the day. Sales had been slow for the week and this was the last morning in which they might expect any business this week. They also hoped that since the previous night had been the Passover meal many other shops would remain closed today. Since the Elders had called for a special meeting that afternoon to discuss Netzereth's response to what was quickly being mockingly called Jesus' "triumphant entry" into Jerusalem, and the evening would bring the Sabbath, there were just a few hours of profitable work time today.

Jesse was helping Jacob carry some cloth from the storage closet to the front booth shelves when he asked, "Father are you planning to attend the meeting this afternoon and may I go as well?

"Yes I'll be going but it will be too dangerous for you to go my son." Jacob placed his bundle of cloth on a shelf and turned toward Jesse and placed his hands on his son's shoulders. He looked him in the eyes and continued. "I want you to stay home with your mother. I intend to speak up for Jesus. It will enrage quite a few people and create a disturbance in the meeting. I must convince them that Jesus is not the threat they think he is. I would prefer that you were safe at home."

"But father, I also want to speak up for the Lamb who takes away the sin of the world."

The look in his son's eyes made him fearful and proud at the same time. "Jesse, the meeting is only for men. You are still a year away from manhood. They would not let you speak, although you do have far greater insight into who Jesus is than all the elders of Netzereth. You need to stay here." Jacob placed his hand on Jesse's cheek. "I love you son and you must care for your mother if anything happens to me."

Emma entered the shop which fronted their home with a load of objects which they thought they could sell this morning since the other shops would be closed. "I also brought out some herbs and vegetables from our garden. I heard that Deborah would not be opening their produce shop this morning. We may pick up some business that would normally go to her shop." She started arranging the produce on a short shelf. "Jesse, could you please open the sales window and bring the sales table out to the street?" Then turning to Jacob she added, "I thought we should put some of our older cloth out on the table where more people can see it. There will be less traffic today and perhaps having it out on the table will help bring more people to our shop."

"Good thinking, I can manage the shop and you can be at the table with your great smile encouraging those walking by to look at the cloth. And Jesse can watch the shop with your help if I should get a tailoring opportunity this morning." Jacob knew that it was his wife's bubbly personality that brought in the most business even though they were the only textile shop in Netzereth and he was the best tailor in the area. He loved her easy way of befriending everyone she met.

"And about this afternoon," Emma added, "I think I will keep the shop open. If all the men are at the town meeting, perhaps a few women will brave shopping our 'Jesus follower's' shop while their men are busy."

"And it will give you a chance to 'gossip' with all your friends." Jacob smiled at his wife. He knew the way Emma always attracted a crowd of women around her with her outgoing personality.

"Well, it will also give me a chance to share with my friends what we discovered about Jesus last night." Emma responded with a wink.

Just then the large wooden sales window on the front of their shop swung up on its rope hinges and Jesse placed the large support poles at each corner which created a shaded area to shop under. He had already moved the table out to the street and had positioned it just in front of the counter top that served as the shops display area.

"Thank you Jesse, you are such a great help to me." Emma straightened Jesse's head covering as she reached over the counter top and then slid her hands down over his ears. "You are growing so fast. Soon you will be starting your own business and getting married, and then what will I do?"

"Mother," Jesse objected as he shook away from her grasp.

Jacob chuckled as he returned to folding cloth. His thoughts then turned to the meeting that afternoon.

"Here son," Emma said, "place these things on the table for me." She handed him a stack of material. "I'll be out there in a minute to help you arrange it properly."

"Woman," Jacob caught Emma's attention before she left the shop area with a voice that signaled the seriousness of his thoughts. "I wish to warn you about saying too much concerning Jesus to your friends today, especially those who have been resistant to the idea of Jesus' messianic role. You know how difficult it is for us three who love Jesus, to accept the idea that he is a sacrificial lamb rather than a king to rid us of Rome, for those who have been taught to revile him, it will be even more difficult."

Emma nodded. "May I ask what you hope to say to the elders this afternoon?"

"I will try to convince them to be cautious concerning any action that might bring Rome's attention here. I will remind them that Jesus' actions in Jerusalem on the first day of this week have not yet brought Rome to Netzereth and may not ever. If I need to, I will point out the facts that we discussed last night and remind them of The Prophet's word concerning a suffering servant of the Almighty. And, if I can, I will speak of his demonstrations of love to everyone he meets and how even the gentiles recognize his special relationship with the Almighty."

"Oh, be careful husband. That was the subject that led him to be taken to the cliffs of town and almost thrown from the heights. I do not wish you to be harmed." Her fear was evident in her eyes and she needed to blink away tears that began to form.

"I will be careful dear, but we are already known to be followers of Jesus. If I don't speak up for him it will be seen as unusual and I would not be able to look Jesus in the eyes next time I see him. Besides Rabbi Isaiah will be there and although he doesn't agree with us, he will not abide by any action that causes harm to the people of Netzereth. I will be safe unless a more militant faction gets control of the leadership."

The face of Matthan, Rabbi Isaiah's apprentice, came to Jacob's mind. A shiver ran down his back and he could see that his words had concerned Emma as well. He sent a silent prayer up to the One asking for wisdom. A particularly interesting story about Jesus came to his mind.

"I think I will share a story I heard about Jesus on my last trip to Tyre. Do you remember me telling you about the woman who spoke to Jesus about her sick child?"

Emma tilted her head with a quizzical look and shook her head. Jacob continued, "She was desperate, so I was told, to get next to Jesus and ask him to heal her daughter. It seems an evil spirit had overcome the little girl and no one was able to control her when the evil spirit was active. The man who told me the story knew the family personally and was aware of several times that the girl was close to killing herself because of the evil spirit."

Emma shook her head. "That poor family, that had to be unbearable for them. What did the mother do?"

"Well, she tried to get close to Jesus but the crowd was so thick around him she couldn't get to him. So she yelled. She yelled with everything in her. The crowd around her thought she had become possessed because she was like a wild dog that keeps barking when you come into his territory. She was non-stop, 'Son of David, have mercy, have mercy.' My friend told me it was rather embarrassing the way this woman kept yelling and behaving as no woman should. But she had no shame."

"Of course not, husband, her little girl was in deadly turmoil. You know you should never cross a mother and her cubs."

"Yes, well it seems that everyone was trying to prevent her from approaching Jesus. Even one or two of his disciples asked Jesus to send her away because she was making such a nuisance of herself. Then Jesus stopped walking and said to his disciples, but loud enough for all the gentiles around him to hear, 'I was sent only to the lost sheep of Israel.'"

"Wow, I imagine that statement didn't go over so well."

"My friend tells me that it started an argument between those near Jesus and his disciples. And Jesus just watched as the crowd got thinner. The gentiles were offended by the attitude that Jesus' disciples had toward them and many left. But that gave an opportunity for this woman to press forward and she eventually got to Jesus and fell to his feet and said, 'Lord, help me. My daughter is suffering from demon-possession.' Jesus looked down at her and said, 'It's not right to take the children's bread and toss it to the dogs.'"

"Her dog impression must have been amazing." Emma started laughing.

"I think what Jesus was referring to and what I hope to enlighten the assembly of this afternoon is that Jesus knows that as the Netzer of the Almighty his priority is first and foremost to the Children of Israel. Jesus is, was, and always has been concerned that Israel be saved from their troubles. His words when he taught here in Netzereth were not meant to dismiss the Almighty's love for Israel but rather to make us jealous for the Almighty by showing that He also cares for the Gentiles."

"I hope they can see that fact, husband. But the elders are so worked up about those statements of Jesus when he was here last, that I fear nothing will sway them from their current path." Emma sighed and slowly shook her head, then quickly brightened and asked, "So what happened with the woman?"

"Oh she was clever." Jacob's smile became wide as he shared the story. "She saw the kindness in Jesus' eyes and said, 'Yes Lord, but even the dogs get the crumbs under the table. All I need is a crumb.' Jesus smiled at her and said, 'You are correct and your daughter is healed.' She ran away screaming 'thank you' all the way. When I heard the story, my friend said that the little girl had been without that demon for four months and the family was beginning to recover their joy. They were also attending a synagogue regularly in Tyre."

"That is a great story, Jacob. I need to share that story with Hadassah. I wish she would ask for healing. I know Jesus would not refuse her."

The couple's enjoyment of sharing stories about Jesus was interrupted by a shout from their son.

"Mother, can you come out here?"

Both Jacob and Emma looked out of the shop window to see three women standing by the table Jesse had put the cloth on. "It might be a good day after all." Emma smiled to Jacob as she walked around the counter to greet the shoppers.

James was polishing a portion of the unfinished synagogue limestone pillar in his courtyard but his mind wasn't on the work. A public debate in the synagogue was scheduled for the afternoon and his mind kept running various scenarios of what might happen. Isaiah seemed to be sympathetic to the family of Jesus if not Jesus himself. Perhaps James could wield his influence as the master stonemason of Netzereth to sway Isaiah and a majority of the men of Netzereth to not take any rash actions against Jesus or his few followers in the village. But what is the clout of a stonemason, master or not, in comparison to teachers of righteousness like Matthan and Isaiah and most of the elders of the village?

He knew Isaiah to be a non-violent man who preferred to influence people by his wit and charm rather than by edict and force. But Matthan was another story. He represented a large group of men who either feared Rome enough or hated Jesus enough to turn the afternoon's discussion into an ugly devastating dispute. But then again, perhaps, there were enough men of even temperament and moderate viewpoints that could keep the discussion fair, open and congenial.

"Humph, fat chance."

"Fat chance of what husband?"

"Oh, you startled me Hadassah" She was standing behind him holding Sarah on one hip. "How long have you been there?"

"Long enough to know that you aren't really accomplishing anything on your project. Would you like to take a break and talk about it?" Sarah reached out a hand for James and beckoned by grabbing at air.

James couldn't resist. He put down his tools and took Sarah in his arms. "You know," James spoke to Hadassah over his shoulder as he turned away from her and walked to the bench in the center of the courtyard, "I would be getting a lot more done and life would be a lot less stressful if Jesus had just stayed here in Netzereth and lived a normal life."

"I don't think he was meant to live a 'normal' life." Hadassah sat next to James on the bench and played with Sarah's hair as Sarah and James made googly eyes at each other. "Besides, as we discussed yesterday, we tried to get him to come home and that was a disaster."

"Well he brought it on himself." James quickly snapped and startled little Sarah who put on a pout. "His words about family and followers made the divide between us greater.

He told us in so many words that we were no longer family to him."

Hadassah took Sarah into her lap and began to comfort her. "I was there James. I heard what he said and it hurt me as well. But as I have been thinking about it, over the past day, I wonder if we have misinterpreted what he said."

"I don't think so. It was clear that he saw his followers as his mother and brothers and sisters. That left us out in the cold, literally. We were not invited into the house and we were sent away without our brother who was making a fool of himself and needed our guidance and help."

"You are correct master."

Hadassah's response startled James. He knew he was right, but the way she said it, although perfectly natural for most women to address their husbands, was not the way they had built their relationship.

"What are you thinking woman?"

Hadassah smiled softly and looked down at their daughter as she spoke.

"James, we went there to save Jesus. We believed he was making a fool of himself and we went with a goal of bringing him home to talk some sense into him. Don't you think he knew our motives? He is obviously still convinced that he is on the right track for his role as the Netzer Messiah, and he believed it then."

"What are you saying? That we were wrong to care about him and the reputation he was creating?"

Hadassah paused, took a deep breath and continued. "James, you are a great stone mason and artist. Look at that column you have built for the new front porch of the synagogue. When you were designing the crown of the column, I could not see the beauty that you were able to chisel out of the limestone, but I trusted you and supported your work. What if others in the village came and said you were doing it all wrong and that you should quit your work and become a farmer instead." James bristled and began to reply, but Hadassah quickly continued. "And then suppose that Joseph, your apprentice, supported your work, continued to follow your lead, listened and obeyed your instructions. Who would you say is really in the know about what you are doing? The many who found fault in your work or the one who supported your vision?

"But we are his family. Doesn't that count for something? He turned us away."

"He told us 'no' to our request that he return with us before we even asked. He did not disown us. Remember he left you in charge of this family. And your mother who is out there right now following him also told you to be the pillar of this family and keep it together. He loves you James, but you can't ask him to be what he isn't. You can't ask him to live a normal life."

"Oh, I can ask." James looked into the distance and slowly shook his head. And then slowly realizing that his wife had spoken truth, he added. "And I can also beat my head against a wall. And I would get the same result. Jesus will continue to be Jesus and I will have a splitting headache."

Hadassah stood with Sarah and bent down to kiss James on the top of his head. "I love you my master. I will now go and prepare your lunch. Perhaps that will help your headache."

James smiled and watched her walk to their room talking to Sarah about lunch. "If only all problems could be solved with a good meal." Then he nodded, stood up and went back to the column and mumbled. "But it's a start."

Matthan entered the house and saw his mentor sitting at the table with the scroll of Isaiah open in front of him. He looked pale and was breathing heavily.

"Master, are you well?"

"Oh do not worry about me my son." Isaiah responded as he rolled up the scroll, kissed it, and placed it on the shelf with two other scrolls. "It is just a bit too hot for me today. Come and sit. We must discuss the events of this afternoon."

Matthan sat and waited for Isaiah to begin the discussion, but a minute had passed with nothing said. So he began, "I believe the goal of today's assembly should be to create a plan which will demonstrate to the Romans that the Netzerim are not supporters of the false prophet Jesus."

"I agree. But we must present a plan to the elders that they will accept today. Time is short. We have no idea how

Jesus' actions in Jerusalem this week may have inflamed the imperialistic passions of the Romans. If we emerge from this meeting not having made a decision we will have wasted a day and then the Sabbath will come and another day will be gone. The Romans will not hesitate to act if they believe we are a treasonous village."

"That is why we must act decisively against Jesus and his followers in our midst." Matthan paused briefly and continued carefully, knowing this would be a difficult subject for Isaiah. "I have been speaking with some of the other elders and prominent men of the Netzerim. We believe we are at a crucial point in the life of the Netzerim and we must act now to cleanse our sect of those who have abandoned the faith of our fathers. We believe we have the voices on the ruling council to excommunicate the followers of Jesus among us and we have men who are willing to act for the faith by eliminating the pretender Jesus."

"And how do you propose to identify those who have been secretly following Jesus? No Matthan, what you are proposing will only tear the community apart. You must remember that unlike you, many of these people grew up with Jesus. They heard the stories of his birth. They watched him mature and impress his neighbors. They love his family. Yes they are outwardly obedient to the law and the elders but their hearts cheer for the man they watched grow up here. And you propose that someone go and assassinate this man who many wish still lived among us?"

"Actually the thought is that someone with a bit more clout could go to the leaders in Jerusalem, who we know would love to rid themselves of Jesus, and provide them with convincing information that would lead to his arrest and execution. In fact, based on what we know of Jesus' triumphant entry, it would not be a stretch to convince even the Roman authorities to execute him for treason."

"You seek a miracle. You know how the leaders in Jerusalem view us. We have all heard the slurs they speak about Galileans and Netzereth in particular. 'Can any good thing come out of Netzereth?' There is no one with enough clout to go and speak with the Sanhedrin in Jerusalem." Isaiah heaved heavily as he finished his rebuttal.

"I respectfully disagree Master." Matthan responded softly and thoughtfully. "You have the clout. You are the head teaching Elder of our village. And you were the teacher of Jesus when he was a child here in Netzereth." Matthan's voice became more excited as he continued. "If you were to go and share how all of Netzereth repudiates the heretic's claim to the throne, they would welcome the report you bring. They would see the opportunity they are looking for to denounce Jesus to the Romans and ask for his crucifixion based on his treasonous triumphant entry in Jerusalem."

"But all of Netzereth does not repudiate Jesus' claim to the throne of David." Isaiah looked at Matthan in confusion.

"That is why those who do not agree with us must be excommunicated. Their names will be removed from the rolls of the Netzerim. They will no longer be called 'Righteous Ones'. And their lands and homes in the village will be confiscated and given to the poor among us. And the act of driving these followers of Jesus from our midst will be evidence to the Romans that we do not support Jesus' claim as king." Matthan finished his explanation of the plan with a smile knowing that the plan was forceful enough to do the job, but also not so strong as to rile Isaiah's sensitivities. It did remove the threat of Roman reprisals, or at least give them pause to think about Netzereth's role in Jesus' claim. It did punish those who still blindly followed Jesus without causing them physical harm. And it could ultimately rid them of Jesus altogether.

Isaiah closed his eyes and sat quietly for a minute before speaking. "Matthan, have you devised a way to know who to excommunicate? I will not tolerate punishing the innocent."

"We know that Jacob and his family follow the false prophet. At the assembly today we will allow him to speak on behalf of Jesus. One of the Elders has already agreed to feign being convinced by his arguments thus giving more secret followers courage to reveal themselves. If all goes as planned we will eliminate most of the heretics and give good warning to those who waver between the truth and the lie."

Isaiah sat quietly for a while and Matthan was not sure which way the decision would turn out. Finally Isaiah said, "Okay I will agree to this plan but will stop it as soon as I believe it harms the community of the Righteous Ones."

Matthan smiled and said, "I am pleased Rabbi that you have seen the value in this course of action. But please rest before the assembly. You do not look well and your presence is very important at the meeting."

"Yes, I will rest. Please call me when it is time to get ready to go to the assembly." Isaiah stood and started to the door which led through the courtyard and to his bedchamber, then turned at the door and asked, "Which Elder will be feigning interest in Jacob's argument?"

"Elder Jeremiah."

CHAPTER 7

(Friday Afternoon)

The synagogue was full. Every man of the village was there. James and his three brothers stood near the rear of the room and James was surprised to see that Jacob was near the front. In James' estimation, Jacob seemed to be surrounded by those whom he knew to be sympathetic to Jesus' claim as the Netzer Messiah. Although there were others that James thought might be sympathetic to Jesus, it was clear that three or four of the more vocal Jesus supporters were around Jacob.

"Attention brothers." Isaiah began from the bema. "We have all come together to seek a solution to the situation we find ourselves in this week. Everybody is welcome and all men are encouraged to speak their minds. I personally guarantee that every viewpoint will be heard by the elders and we will arrive at a solution which will protect Netzereth and all the Righteous from the threats that confront us today. We have already taken requests from a number of you for permission to speak. Among those making requests is Elder

Jeremiah. So out of respect to his position in the community I am asking him to speak first."

James noticed that Isaiah was not his jovial self which may have been due to the topic of the meeting. But James thought there was more to it than just the serious mood in the room. Isaiah also walked slower than usual as he moved to his seat on the bema making room for Elder Jeremiah who briskly walked up the steps of the bema.

"Men of Netzereth," Jeremiah began, "these are serious times and we must not move hastily or without proper thought. I was one of those who enthusiastically welcomed the news of Mary and Joseph when they explained the Almighty's call on their lives. My father's father taught me as a young child that the words of the prophets spoke of the Netzer Messiah coming from the loins of King David, that He would be a leader, that He would sit on the throne of David. Therefore I am very interested to hear if perchance we have been too quick to deny Jesus as the true king of Israel."

The crowd of men in the synagogue began to grumble and one voice rang out, "He is not my king."

Isaiah quickly rose from his chair and bellowed, "Silence. Give your respect to Elder Jeremiah." He then collapsed back into his chair as if exhausted from the exertion. Matthan jumped up onto the bema and knelt by his mentor. After a few whispers were exchanged, Matthan stood up and addressed the assembly.

"Righteous men, our Rabbi Isaiah has asked that I continue the meeting under his authority as he is a bit tired.

So I must insist that we all remain orderly and allow each speaker their time to share. Right now it is Elder Jeremiah's turn. Please continue Jeremiah."

Jeremiah continued with a concerned look on his face. "I realize that much of what we hear today will not be welcome statements. But we must hear those who disagree with us so we can better understand how we can respond to our present situation. As I have already said, I welcomed the news of Joseph and Mary with joy. But since then I have seen their eldest son grow into a man who does not embody the principles on which the Righteous Ones have built our many communities throughout Israel not the least of these being this village of the Netzerim. I want to hear from those who still put some hope in Jesus how they would answer these questions." Jeremiah proceeded to count off the questions on his fingers. "Why did Jesus abandon us and move to Capernaum? Has he joined the sect of the Pharisees? Why did Jesus compare us to the rebellious tribes during the reign of the wicked king Ahab and the ministries of Elijah and Elisha? Why has He spurned the openings he has had to raise an army and rid us of our oppressors? Why has he now announced his kingly role by a 'triumphant entry' into Jerusalem? Does he want to bring down Rome's wrath on us without defending us?"

"James, those are pretty good questions." Judas whispered into his brother's ear from behind. James nodded as he scanned the crowd to see if anyone was going to dare answering the questions Elder Jeremiah had posed.

Matthan stepped up next to Jeremiah and looked directly at Jacob. "I have been made aware of those who have asked to speak and I believe one man in particular may have some possible answers. Jacob, would you like to respond to these questions?"

Something isn't right, James thought. Matthan is a bit too cordial to Jacob.

James turned to face his brothers. "Do you see what I see? Do you think Isaiah finally got through to Matthan and convinced him to soften his approach?"

"I believe in miracles." Joseph replied.

"Looks more like a trap to me." Simon added.

James turned back to the front in time to see Jacob ascending the bema. Matthan had a smile on his face... but it was a mischievous one.

"My friends, my brothers, Righteous Ones of the Netzerim, I humbly ask you to hear me out as I share what I know of Jesus and his teaching." Jacob spoke with his usual calming but confident voice and James was eager to hear what he had to say. And it seemed others were also ready to listen. The whole room fell silent as Jacob paused to collect his thoughts.

"I will attempt to answer Elder Jeremiah's questions, but I must start from the beginning. The older men here will remember the excitement of Joseph and Mary as they shared the announcements the angels brought to them about the birth of the Netzer Messiah. I was just a child at the time but I remember the stories my father shared with me and I confirmed with my childhood friend, Jesus. They both explained that when Joseph first heard of Mary's pregnancy he considered calling off the wedding and encouraging Mary's family to send her to distant relatives in Sidon to bear the child and leave it there. But then he experienced an amazing thing. An angel of the Almighty appeared to him in a dream and explained that the prophesies concerning the Netzer would be coming true through Mary and that he was to raise the Messiah as his own. What our fathers have always taught us, what the Essenes in every community of the Righteous Ones believes, what every descendant of David had prayed would happen in his family, was now coming to fruition through Joseph and Mary."

James noticed a number of heads nodding in agreement with Jacob's words. However, most of those heads were near the bema where Jacob had been surrounded by others who still wished for Jesus' claims to be true.

Jacob continued, "Of course they shared their joy with others of like faith. And my father tells me, all the Netzerim were in support of them. Then the birth itself with the trip to the city of David and the army of angels appearing to the shepherds confirmed their joy. Even others not of the Essene sect spoke of the child's importance when they took him to the Temple for his dedication. Even Herod saw the birth as a threat to him and tried to kill the child but again Joseph saved the boy by heeding the message of another dream and escaping to Egypt until King Herod was gone. These facts alone should have us all convinced that Jesus is the Netzer Messiah. But then the family moved back home to Netzereth and we all watched him grow. Has anyone ever seen a child so obedient and special? His grasp of the Torah amazed even the teachers of the Torah in Jerusalem. And then one of our own respected teachers, whom many see as a prophet of the Almighty, John the Baptizer, identified him as the one to come."

"Jacob, we know all this. The problem is that he is not acting like the Netzer now." The rebuttal came from Gurion, one of the men James knew as a fair man.

"I know, Gurion. That brings me to the questions that Elder Jeremiah raised. They are fair questions. 'Why did Jesus move to Capernaum?' I know that Capernaum is the seat of Pharisaical teaching in Galilee. But perhaps his leaving Netzereth for Capernaum was due more to audience than ideologies. Capernaum is a larger town on the banks of the Sea of Galilee. It is on the main road that leads North and South through our land. It is a city of commerce and fishing. Netzereth has 400 people at most, and half of them are children! We are off any main road. The Netzer must have an audience to teach about the ways of the Kingdom."

James recognized the logic of Jacob's answer.

"Elder Jeremiah's next question is, 'Did he join the Pharisees?' I doubt it, but if he considers himself a Pharisee it may be because they have the ears of the populous. Our sect is the smallest in the land, in fact many Jews consider us strange and fanatical. You all know this. Being a Pharisee allows him to travel to many towns and teach in their synagogues. And besides being a Pharisee isn't so bad. I have even heard it said right here in this synagogue that we would do well to do what the Pharisees teach but not follow their example."

Matthan interrupted, "That may have been said but the wise man knows that bad company corrupts a person."

"But, Matthan, have you heard Jesus interact with the Pharisees? He points out their wickedness every chance he gets. If he considers himself a Pharisee, they certainly do not agree with him."

"Jacob, I am beginning to see and appreciate your perspective and perhaps others also agree with you." Jeremiah smiled and then added inquisitively. "I am intrigued and am anxious to hear how you would answer my next question. Why did he compare us, his own people, with the rebellious tribes of Elijah and Elisha's ministry?"

Murmurs rippled through the synagogue. This is the crux of the matter thought James. These people are hurting. They heard rejection from Jesus that day. In fact, that was also the feeling he had been dealing with this whole time. James could now see it in his life more clearly now that he saw it in others. His big brother whom he idolized as a child and young man left him. That is what really hurt. Intellectually he understood the reasons, but the pain was still there. And how did he deal with the pain? He looked for flaws in his brother; his move to Capernaum, his statement about family when they went to bring him home, his distancing from Essene life. All these things were just excuses to validate the pain of rejection he felt when Jesus left. James turned to share his self discovery with his brothers but noticed that their attention was glued to the bema. James snapped out of his reverie to hear the shout from the assembly.

"He did say it. He said the gentiles deserve to have God's favor and not us."

Jacob stood there a bit shell shocked, as the accusations flew at him.

Matthan stepped forward and attempted to silence the crowd. "Men please, we must listen to understand. Jacob has already prefaced his remarks with the admission that he was not here the day Jesus spoke in this synagogue. And his answer is based on conjecture about what Jesus meant. Perhaps there is someone else who can speak to this?" Matthan looked in the direction of James.

James was about to step forward when Saul bounded up to the bema. James knew that Saul was one of the few ardent supporters of Jesus who kept his loyalty hidden, until now.

"I was there." Saul started. "I heard what he said and I believe I know what he meant."

Matthan smiled. "Thank you Saul. You may speak."

"He was given the scroll of Isaiah to read. He read the messianic passage, 'The Spirit of the Lord is upon me, because he anointed me to preach the gospel to the poor. He has sent me to proclaim release to the captives, and recovery of sight to the blind, to set free those who are downtrodden. To proclaim the favorable year of the Lord.' And then he closed the scroll and sat down to teach us."

Saul paused and asked, "How many of you here know what line was next in the prophecy about the work of the anointed?" Many men in the room nodded their heads and even whispered the next line to their neighbor.

"Our Essene rabbis have taught us well. From childhood we are all taught the prophecies of the Netzer Messiah. 'Then a Netzer will spring from the stem of Jesse and a branch from his roots will bear fruit. And the Spirit of the Lord will rest on Him.' The line that Jesus left out of his reading is probably the most important line to all of us living in Galilee and Judea today. It speaks of the Almighty's vengeance. It says '…to proclaim the favorable year of the Lord and the day of vengeance of our God; to comfort all who mourn.' And we all are looking for that vengeance to be meted out with justice on the Romans who enslave us and kill us with their taxes and armies. But Jesus did not read that line. Instead he sat down and said, 'Today, this Scripture is fulfilled."He then went on to teach how he was the anointed and how he fulfilled the passage he read. But some among us wanted the unread passage fulfilled. And Jesus refused to speak on that subject. This angered some in the crowd. They rejected his claim to be the Netzer. They demanded a sign, even though as my brother Jacob has already pointed out, he gave us many signs at his birth and growing up with us. It was then that he reminded us all of how Elijah and Elisha were treated by the rebellious tribes of their day. He reminded us that when The Name is rejected by His own people He shows loving kindness to the gentiles. This enraged many of you. He refused to speak of the destruction of the Romans and instead spoke of kindness to them. And for his kindness to gentiles you wished to throw him off the village cliff."

By now Saul was enraged himself and the fire of passion spread across the room again. Suddenly encouraged by Saul's bravery, other supporters of Jesus began to yell back at those who were shouting at Saul and Jacob. Shouts turned to pushing and pushing to fighting among a few of the more boisterous men.

Isaiah stood up and with Matthan's help, brought back a semblance of peace. But the tension in the room was so thick. James noticed that Simon had moved closer to the group of Jesus supporters and so he started making his way over to him to pull him back.

"I wish to speak." The voice was that of Nathaniel. "I agree with Saul,' at that moans and shouts began again and Nathaniel had to quiet them down with hand motions and bellowed, "I agree with Saul that Jesus does coddle the gentiles, and for this reason we know he is not the Netzer Messiah. Thus we must doubt the signs of his so-called miraculous birth. We know that there is only one way a 13 year old woman can get pregnant. Either Joseph was a liar and fornicator, or Mary was a harlot."

James caught Simon by the sleeve of his robe and motioned him and the two other brothers to meet him outside.

"I see that the ones who can answer that riddle are leaving." Nathaniel yelled after the brothers. "Tell me James is your father a fornicator or is your mother a harlot?"

James pushed his brothers out the door and turned to respond with a stabbing word of his own but all he could do was stare back at Nathaniel in anger. Frustrated with his own lack of a response, he turned and stormed out of the assembly.

Isaiah bellowed from the bema. "Men this has gotten out of control. We are not here to attack each other. We are here to resolve together what must be done to save Netzereth."

James walked away from the synagogue knowing that he could add nothing to what was already said without stirring up passions again.

"Nathaniel and Saul, please return to your places in the assembly. Jacob, I have sensed that there is something else you wish to say which may help us. After you have your say I want to open the floor to others who wish to speak." Isaiah put his arm around Jacob and smiled, then hobbled back to his seat.

Jacob began haltingly, "I am not sure if this is the right time to share this but it does have bearing on what Nathaniel and Saul have brought up. We have always been looking for a Netzer who would rule as a king like his father David. That would necessitate the removal of foreign occupiers, and he would bring peace between men by raising a protective army, and he would free the slaves from their gentile oppressors. But, what if the Netzer is not that kind of Messiah? The prophets often spoke of a suffering servant. Isn't it possible that Jesus intends to be not a king but rather a Passover Lamb? Remember what John the Baptizer said when he identified Jesus as the Netzer Messiah, 'Behold the Lamb of God who takes away the sin of the world.'"

"Where did you hear that? That's a lie."

Jacob responded to the voice from the crowd. "It is what has been reported by some of John's disciples. And if this is true, Jesus does not wish to bring the Romans down on us. Instead what has happened in Jerusalem recently has not had any effect on us here in Netzereth because Jesus is using that event to lead, possibly, to his death as a Passover Lamb to bring peace between man and The One, and free us from our slavery to sin."

"Jacob, you are speaking of things you do not know." Isaiah almost giggled as he approached Jacob. "You have not studied the Law, Prophets, and Writings as I have. The Suffering Servant of the Prophets is Israel. All who follow The Almighty faithfully and suffer for their faithfulness are anointed by The One to be a light to the nations. Jesus is not a Passover Lamb. One man can not die for the sins of another man. That goes against all that the Scriptures teach." At that Isaiah could not hold in his laughter and let out a loud guffaw and leaned on Jacob for support. Then he leaned heavier on him. Then he collapsed on him. Jacob lowered Isaiah to the floor and looked up with surprise at Matthan who came and put his head on Isaiah's chest to listen for a heartbeat.

"Thank you Emma for sending Jessie to watch my children during the meeting. It was so wonderful to shop and visit with all the women this afternoon without having to worry about them." Hadassah and Emma were walking briskly back to Hadassah's home after Hadassah had helped Emma close the shop for the day.

"Your welcome dear. You know I did it for selfish reasons. I wanted to spend time with you and share what we have been thinking about Jesus being a Passover Lamb."

"Yes I know. I love spending time with you and talking about Jesus as well. But I don't like the ideas you have shared with me. They scare me more than the talk of Roman soldiers attacking Netzereth. Emma I hope you are wrong. I believe Jesus is the Netzer. And James is close to believing as well. If Jesus were to die, I am not sure that any kind of study of the prophesies could convince James that it was part of The Almighty's plan. Jesus' death would just drive James further away from the truth." Hadassah suddenly stopped and faced Emma. "You see James loves his older brother more than even he knows. Jesus' death would kill James."

The two women hugged and Emma whispered, "The One works in mysterious ways my friend. Let us pray that He will work a miracle through all of this."

Hadassah released her hug and began walking slowly toward home again. "Emma, I pray that every day." She sighed and smiled at her good friend.

"Hadassah," Emma thoughtfully asked, "you said that you believe that Jesus is the Netzer Messiah. I have never heard you say that before. What brought you to that decision?"

"Oh, I guess I have always believed it. Jesus always loved me like a sister and he has always proven himself to be honest and of sound mind. So if he claims to be my Messiah, I believe him."

"But you went with James and his brothers and tried to get him to quit his ministry. I have even heard your family talk about it as an attempt to 'save our crazy brother from himself'?"

"Yes, I went. But I went as James' obedient woman. James would not want me to share my belief in Jesus with him. We have recently had many conversations concerning Jesus in which I have challenged James to think in a different way about his brother. But that is as far as I dare go as a wife."

"I don't think I would have the control to keep still." Emma smiled.

"No you probably could not." Hadassah laughed. She reached for the gate handle of her home's courtyard and said, "My mother once told me that the best way to change your husband's mind about anything is to feed him well, care for him, and serve him, until he believes like you do, and thinks it is his idea in the first place."

Both women were laughing as they entered the courtyard and all three children came running to them.

"How is my Schmeeka?" Hadassah picked up Joshua and gave him a big hug.

"Jesse taught me a new game! Let's show her Jesse."

Joshua jumped down from his mother's embrace and held out his arms to Jesse. Jesse handed Sarah to Hadassah. Then he took hold of Joshua's wrists as did Joshua of his. He began to spin in circles and soon Joshua's feet left the ground and he was screaming with delight.

Hadassah started screaming too. "OHH be careful. That's enough, that's enough."

Jesse slowly stopped spinning and released Joshua when he was on his own feet. They both stumbled a bit and laughed at each other.

"I get a little dizzy doing that." Jesse confessed.

"That is a good reason not to do it anymore." Hadassah quipped.

"Aw, Eema, it's fun."

"Looks dangerous to me Joshua. How about we all sit down to a snack of bread and olive oil?"

Emma reached out for her son and gave Jesse a hug. "Jacob has been giving Jesse rides like that since he was two years old." She smiled at Hadassah. "But perhaps it would be wise to have a snack right now." She winked at Hadassah.

Hadassah gathered the bread and oil as Emma helped arrange the chairs around the table. They had just taken their first bite when the men returned from the assembly.

"Is the meeting over already?" Hadassah asked.

"It would have been over sooner if James hadn't have stopped me." Simon said sullenly as he headed for his work-room and shut the door.

"What was that about? Did everything go okay? Is Simon okay?" Hadassah rose and stood before James grabbing his strong arms.

"What happened at the meeting?" Emma stood and placed her hands on Jesse's shoulders as he stood in front of her.

"It was rough, and they will probably be at it till sundown." Joseph said. "Oh bread. I'm famished." He sat in Hadassah's place and took a bite of the warm bread.

"Emma, your husband spoke well and shared some insights that caused even some of the Elders to question what they believe about our brother." Judas stated as he headed for the room he shared with Simon and Joseph. "I want to read Isaiah's prophesy that Jesus read when he was here in Netzereth."

Both women now looked at James with pleading eyes.

"The meeting is still going on. We left because the accusations were getting too personal." James sat and took a piece of bread. "Jacob and Saul spoke wonderfully of why they believe Jesus to be the Netzer. They had a bit of backlash from some in the crowd. At one point it seemed the meeting would end in a war within the synagogue but Isaiah stood in the gap to calm everyone down. Even Matthan seemed to be more willing to entertain the claims of Jesus. I don't think we need to worry. Nothing will be decided today. And Isaiah will protect all the Netzerim, even those who disagree with him."

"Is my husband still there? Asked Emma.

Suddenly it became dark. Simon and Judas came out of their room and joined the others looking up at the sun as it was being blackened.

"What is happening?" Hadassah asked.

Sarah started crying and everyone gathered together.

"I have read of this happening before. I have always heard that it is a sign of bad things." Judas shared.

"Hadassah, take the children into our room. Joseph, please escort Emma and Jesse home, I am sure Jacob will be there soon. Judas and Simon and I will go back to the meeting and see if anyone knows what this means." Everyone looked at James with fear. And James also felt fear concerning this omen in the sky. He gave Hadassah and Joshua a hug and said, "Now get going. Everything will be okay."

Emma gave Hadassah a hug goodbye and picked up her shawl from her chair. Everyone watched Hadassah and the children enter the room and then they all turned to leave.

Suddenly there was a frantic knock on the gate and then it burst open. It was Gurion. He was out of breath as he ran up to James.

"James, Isaiah is dead and Jacob has been arrested as the murderer."

CHAPTER 8

S abbath had begun. Sundown brought an end to a tragic day for James, his family, and friends. James had spent the rest of the afternoon trying to visit Jacob who was being held under guard in the synagogue. Emma had pleaded with James, she wanted to go along to see her husband, but James had refused her, knowing that there was very little chance that anyone would be allowed to see Jacob. It turned out that he was right. Matthan and the Netzereth Elders had left strict orders that no one was to see the prisoner while they quickly prepared Isaiah's body for burial before sunset and the beginning of the Sabbath.

The family sat for a quick evening meal which Hadassah had prepared before the sun had disappeared under the western horizon. Joining them were Emma and Jesse, whom James now felt responsible to protect.

"Heavenly Father, we thank you for your provision and your protection. We ask that you remember your children during this day of trouble. Especially care for your servant Jacob and show your goodness in his life. Amen."

James looked at his wife who had just heard the shortest prayer he had ever uttered in her presence. She was reading him as only she could do. He was worried, weary, and frustrated. But he gained strength from her ability to silently help him bear his pain. He then turned to look at Emma and his heart broke. Emma just stared at her empty plate. Her whole body shook as she intermittently sobbed. Jesse sat next to her trying to comfort her with hugs and hand holding. Every one else also sat or ate quietly. Even Joshua and Sarah seemed to understand the soberness of the night.

"James, do you believe my husband will be safe tonight at the synagogue?" Emma's question was so soft he almost didn't hear it.

James nodded, "I have a personal assurance from Elder Ezra and Gurion that they will not let anything happen to him. I trust those two men. He will be safe."

"Another important question my brother, is whether we will be safe here in Netzereth?" James looked at him and Simon continued. "Jesus' actions have enraged this town's Elders and men of influence. They convened a meeting to determine how to deal with the obvious threat it has brought on us from the Romans and at that meeting the most outspoken follower of Jesus had many new, and I suppose, heretical things to say about Jesus." Everyone looked at Emma who just continued to sob quietly. "And then the person you said would protect us from hot-headed men dies in the meeting while leaning on Jacob. We are in big trouble and it is time we either stand and fight or get out of town. We are not safe here."

"I agree." Joseph added. "Although I don't think we have the resources or men to fight for our defense. We need to leave Netzereth. We can go to our cousins in Cana or to Gamla like Simon suggested earlier."

"Or we could flee to Joppa and catch a ship for Tarshish." James said more forcefully than he intended. Emma looked at him with surprise and then quickly pushed back her chair and retreated to the great room which Hadassah had prepared for her and Jesse to sleep in that night. Jesse followed his mother.

"No Emma, you misunderstand," James called after her. "We are not going anywhere."

"Really, husband, your tongue is a spark that can set a whole forest on fire. I'll go see if I can help her calm down." Hadassah picked up Sarah and followed Emma and Jesse.

James sighed and shook his head at his own stupidity. Then seeing Joshua still at the table, he said, "Son, please go with your mother and help her with Sarah for a while."

"Yes, abba." Joshua slipped out of his chair and ran after Hadassah catching her robe just as she was entering the great room.

The brothers all sat silently for a minute, each one thinking of the predicament in which they found themselves. And finally Judas spoke.

"Of course being like Jonah and running from what the One has commanded us to do would be foolish. But tell me brother, why shouldn't we quietly slip away to a safer town?"

"You are all men and can make decisions for yourselves on how to best proceed for yourselves individually. But please hear me out before you make any final decision." James looked at each of his brothers getting an affirming nod from each one, although Simon's also came with an eye roll. "When our brother left Netzereth to begin his teaching, he left me in charge of the family, a role I was not exactly desirous of, but here we are. As leader of the household I have taken responsibility of Jacob's woman and son. The Prophet Isaiah tells us that the Almighty desires us to watch over the widows and fatherless in our midst. And although Jacob is not dead, he soon will be if we do nothing. The One often asked our patriarchs to prove their faith in Him by acting on what they believe. Faith in the Almighty without action is worthless. So I intend to do all I can to help Jacob in his time of need. And besides, I do not desire to be the caregiver of Emma and Jesse long term. My own family is work enough." James smiled softly so his brothers knew he intended humor.

"If the three of us left, your great burden could be lighter my brother."

James looked at Joseph and quipped, "Yes, yes it would." And then he added after a short pause. "But brothers, I am asking you to stay. I need your help. This family has always pulled together when going through tough times. When our father died, although we were still very young men, we each stepped up to the challenge by providing what we could to encourage each other and our mother in the difficult months that followed. When we heard how Jesus was conducting himself in public, we all went together to deal with the situation. We are a family and I am asking that the family stay together during this trial and work to solve the problem, not run from it."

"Brother, surely the Almighty doesn't ask us to do what is foolish. Staying in Netzereth is tremendously foolish. We can take Emma and Jesse with us. We can protect them as well." Simon paused and then brightened with additional ideas. "And we need not stay away forever, when the mood changes here in Netzereth we can return. Perhaps, as Jacob believes, we have exaggerated the affront to the Romans of Jesus' actions, and all will resolve itself in a couple of weeks."

Everyone looked at Simon with raised eyebrows. "You don't believe that Simon." Then turning to James, Judas added, "But I do agree that a temporary departure may be the wisest thing to do."

"As I have already said, you three are free to leave if you wish. But I am not sure that the Almighty doesn't ask us to do what seems to be foolishness. Didn't it seem foolish for Abraham to sacrifice his son Isaac? It looked foolish for Noah to build an ark in a world with no rain. It was foolish for Elijah to poor water on the sacrifice and ask the One to send fire. It looked foolish for the children of Israel to march around the walls of Jericho. Perhaps it is when we obey the Almighty by doing what seems foolish to men that He shows up in power and makes the obedient wise."

The four of them sat at the table quietly in their own thoughts for a few minutes. As James looked at his brothers he loved them in a way he had never before. He knew that his argument had won the day but not necessarily because of its soundness. Rather his brothers would stay in Netzereth because of their loyalty to him. And with that thought, the memory of what Jesus had said to him on the roof of the homestead three and a half years earlier came rushing back to him. "James, I need you to hold the family together. Promise me." A warmth filled James in remembering Jesus' words and the picture before him. A smile came to his lips. Then he suddenly realized he was hungry and took a bite of the bread on his plate.

That action seemed to rouse his brothers from their own reverie and they all started eating.

Judas was the first to speak. "I would rather look foolish for the Almighty than scared of Matthan and his lap dogs. I'll stay and help you James."

"Hey I'm not afraid of Matthan or even the Romans. I'm with you brother." Simon announced.

Everyone looked at Joseph, who was busy stuffing his face with food. When he realized that all eyes were on him he stopped the stuffing and said with a full mouth, "What?" With the continuing stares he quickly chewed and swallowed and looked at James. "Brother, you knew all along I was staying with you."

James smiled and slapped Joseph's shoulder with his left hand.

"Besides I need you to help me finish that room for my beautiful bride, Zerah."

All four men laughed out loud and began jesting about Joseph and Zerah.

At the doorway of the grand room stood Hadassah, she had heard most of the table conversation. She admired her husband.

"This is not right. This meeting should not be happening on the Sabbath." Ezra's complaint got a few nods from the assembled town elders. All ten of the elders and Matthan had gathered in the synagogue at the request of Matthan and Jeremiah.

"You are right Ezra. Under normal circumstances we would not be meeting, but with the murder of Isaiah and the threat of Roman retribution looming we needed to make some quick decisions."

"What decisions Jeremiah? Nothing that couldn't wait 24 hours? We, as elders of Netzereth, are in violation of His Law. We bring shame on our whole town."

"We are in a dire situation here Ezra." Jeremiah shouted.

Matthan put his hand on Jeremiah's arm to calm him down. Ezra recognized immediately the connection between the two. They had obviously been working together to arrange this unlawful meeting.

Jeremiah took the silent warning well and calmed down before speaking. "There are two issues that need our immediate attention. And who of us would not step up to meet a life and death need of our own family on the Sabbath? Netzereth is our family. The gathering that ended in the murder of our beloved Rabbi never reached its conclusion. I don't believe that a general meeting of all the men of Netzereth would ever come to a solid decision. It is up to us as the leaders of the town to decide how to proceed."

"How is that a life and death decision on the Sabbath? You are twisting the Law to serve your own desires. You are behaving like the Sadducees and Pharisees that have no respect for the One and His Word. I am leaving." Ezra turned to go.

"You may call me names all you want Ezra, but that does not change the fact that our Rabbi is dead and word has gotten to Sepphoris." With a look of derision toward Ezra, Jeremiah continued. "You know that place don't you Ezra? The regional seat of power of Rome where a magistrate sits in authority over this small town we love. Do you remember how he responded when Elder Micah died 6 months ago? Oh, I see you do remember him coming to Netzereth the very next day with 30 soldiers looking for a reason to destroy our role as elders and economically ruin the whole town. It was only by the quick thinking of Isaiah, his winsome character, and the sacrifice of half our market goods to support the magistrate and his soldiers that we survived that visit. We can not afford another visit like that."

Ezra turned around and reluctantly re-joined the meeting. Yes he remembered well that visit from the Sepphoris magistrate. He had lost half of his crops to that "taxation" and if it were not for the quick thinking of his wife who hid their daughter he might have lost his daughter as well to a soldier who had seen her in the market. Perhaps this meeting was a matter of life and death.

Jeremiah continued. "As I was saying, we have two issues to decide. One is how we are going to handle the threat of Rome because of Jesus' 'triumphant entry' into Jerusalem earlier this week. The second is how to handle the loss of Rabbi Isaiah who knew how to phrase things. 'Triumphant entry', that was classic Isaiah."

Almost everyone smiled at the reference to Isaiah's way with words. Ezra was the only one who did not see the humor in the memory.

"First of all we need to affirm Matthan as our Rabbi to take the place of Isaiah. This will go a long way to demonstrating to the Magistrate that we are moving forward and not weakened by the loss of Isaiah. Is that agreeable to everyone?"

All the elders nodded. Although Ezra had doubts about Matthan, he was the heir apparent and there were no other options.

Matthan then took charge of the meeting. "Men, thank you for your affirmation. I will never be able to serve you as well as my predecessor, but I will try. Isaiah was a great man to whom I am indebted for teaching me in wisdom and love for the Righteous Ones of Netzereth." Matthan paused and wiped his damp eyes. He cleared his voice and continued. "I believe I have a solution to our dilemma. If you will allow me to share what is on my heart I will then of course hear your ideas and we can quickly come to a solution that will protect Netzereth and get us home to rest on this Sabbath."

After a short pause and surveying the blank faces of the elders, Matthan continued. "Our major issue is not what we have done but rather what this Jesus has done. We must distance ourselves from any and all connections to him. By doing this we will demonstrate to the Gentile dogs that currently rule us that we are not involved in this plot to overthrow their authority. I propose that we arrest all known and suspected followers of Jesus and put them on trial as quickly as possible. Those that are proven to be sympathizers of the imposter will be excommunicated from the Way of the Righteous Ones and forced to leave Netzereth. Their land and homes will be confiscated and given to the faithful as the elders deem appropriate."

A few of the elders had shocked faces and others nodded in agreement. Ezra was about to object to the plan as unnecessary and outrageous. But before he could speak, Matthan continued.

"I realize that this is drastic action, but when your family is threatened you must act quickly and decisively. And we are being merciful. The Law calls for heretics to be stoned and their memory to be erased from the nation. Our punishment for the guilty will be less harsh and allow them to settle with other Israelites who more closely believe as they do. And I fear the Almighty may not be pleased with the leniency we offer but we can only do what we can do." Matthan paused and shook his bowed head in feigned remorse for those who would be excommunicated.

Jeremiah continued what seemed to Ezra as almost a rehearsed discussion. "I think the plan has merit, but we must act quickly. It has already been several days since the incident in Jerusalem. The Roman army may be on their way to Netzereth as we speak. I suggest we move forward with the plan the day after Sabbath. We can use the trial of Jacob as a method to identify the other followers of the impostor. The trial of Jacob for the murder of Isaiah is scheduled to begin the morning after Sabbath. I am requesting all elders to be present and be prepared to identify possible followers of the impostor Jesus." Then moving forward before any discussion could take place, Jeremiah asked. "Does this plan agree with all of you?"

All the elders nodded their approval except Ezra. But when he saw all the others had been swayed by Jeremiah and Matthan he reluctantly gave assent also.

"Then it is decided."

Jeremiah thanked them all for their service to Netzereth and dismissed them.

A short time later in the home which Matthan now owned by right as the village rabbi, Matthan gathered with "the Leftovers" to talk about the exciting days to come and how each of them would play a part in the removal of heretics from their community.

"Brothers, the meeting of the elders could not have gone better. I am pleased that the omen in the sky that occurred after the death of our Rabbi Isaiah was not a portend of difficulties in convincing the Elders to move forward in dealing with the heretics among us. We have been given the authority to rid ourselves of the followers of Jesus and also rearrange the meager wealth of Netzereth to better serve the purposes of the Netzerim." Matthan smiled broadly as he poured each of his compatriots a cup of wine.

Jeremiah nodded and responded. "I was a little worried about Ezra's reaction to the meeting. He could have swayed some of the opinions if he had spoken up again. Thank you Matthan for reminding me to curb my anger with him. He makes me so mad. I wanted to strangle him right there."

"I'm glad you realized what was happening when I touched your arm. By the way, I am a bit upset with you. The news about the Sepphoris magistrate should have not been a surprise to me. How did he hear of Isaiah's death so quickly? If I had known that information we could have used it better. And I don't like being surprised."

Jeremiah looked over the rim of his cup at Matthan and the others while he took a long drink of wine. Then slowly lowering the cup he said, "The magistrate doesn't know about Isaiah's death. In fact, I believe he is in Caesarea on official business right now. I made it up." A sly smile played across his face.

Matthan's mouth was open in shock and slowly turned to a big smile and a hardy laugh came rolling out. "I am truly amazed. Brothers, we are in the presence of a genius. Here, let me re-fill your cup brother." Matthan filled Jeremiah's cup to the brim and passed the pitcher to Heber and Nathaniel who were surprised by this sudden burst of laughter.

"Let me explain." Matthan continued as the others poured more wine for themselves. "At the beginning of the meeting Elder Ezra was walking out the door and I could see others about to follow him when our friend Jeremiah saved the day by saying that we might get a visit tomorrow from the Sepphoris magistrate. He reminded everyone of the horrible events six months ago and convinced even Ezra to stay and give his assent to our plan. His ruse saved the day. Even I was concerned about the possibility that we would have to deal with the magistrate and his soldiers tomorrow."

All four men laughed out loud at their good fortune.

"I wish I had been there. To see the looks on the Elder's faces as they contemplated a raid from Sepphoris." Heber laughed again and then suddenly stopped.

Matthan noticed that Heber had struck a nerve with Nathaniel.

"I almost wish they would raid. I would kill a few before they ended my life."

"Nathaniel, no one can really understand the pain you have in losing your family to the Gentile dogs but a suicide mission for revenge would be foolhardy." Heber put his hand on Nathaniel's shoulder to calm him and then turned to Matthan. "So what is next?"

"I wish I could say that we can rest and enjoy our Sabbath but we have many things to discuss. So, my friends, let's sit. Listen as I explain what needs to be done." Matthan motioned to the chairs around the table at which just two days earlier they had all shared a Passover meal together.

"I don't know the details you have worked out Rabbi," Jeremiah's use of his official title brought a smile to Matthan's face, "but I am hoping that we could somehow rid ourselves of Elder Ezra in this purge. I think he shows sympathy to the followers of the imposter."

"And his farmland is right next to yours isn't it Elder Jeremiah?" Nathaniel added with a knowing smile.

"Well, now that you mention it. I believe it is." Jeremiah returned the smile.

"I believe that can be arranged Jeremiah. The key to this plan however will rest on the shoulders of Nathaniel and Heber. And, rewarding them for their hard work will also be part of the plan." Matthan looked at the two men. "Are you two prepared to take on a solemn task for the good of the Netzerim?"

The two nodded and then listened to Matthan's plan.

CHAPTER 9

(Saturday Morning)

James and his brothers sat together as usual during morning prayers. But as the Sabbath assembly began they found themselves pulled in separate directions. Judas was led to the scriptorium by Elder Ezra and when they emerged they sat near the front of the assembly. Joseph was called to the side of the assembly hall to speak with Zerah's father, David. They sat together on the right side of the synagogue. Simon found some friends and sat in the back. James immediately sought to speak to Jacob. But after many attempts to get permission to see him he gave up and sat alone in a back corner.

Before sitting he looked up to the divided balcony where the women and children gathered and noticed Hadassah and Emma with the children and nodded to them. Hadassah looked somber and Emma was quietly crying. James sat with a heavy heart and awaited Matthan's opening of the assembly.

"Things couldn't get much worse." James thought as the seconds slowly moved along. He was plagued by the possible outcomes of the current trial they were experiencing, all of

them unbearably dark. Of course he did entertain the thought that Matthan and the village elders would just release Jacob, but that would be kind, and Matthan was definitely not the kind type. So the dark thoughts kept flooding his mind and James could not think of anything else.

Eventually the service began with the call to worship. James sat in silence and let the proceedings just wash over him without engaging in any meaningful thought about what was being said. At one point the assembly stood for the reading of the Torah and the Prophets. Elder Ezra read from the third book of Moses concerning the blessings of obedience and the consequences of disobedience. The passage spoke of the removal of the people from the Promised Land so that the land might have its Sabbath rest.

"Rest" thought James, "will we ever have rest?"

For a few brief years the Jewish people had enjoyed autonomy from foreign control since the return from exile, but for the most part their political history had been a series of despotic rulers from foreign lands. The people of Israel ached for a rest from the Gentiles.

After Elder Ezra had read the proscribed reading from the Torah, Matthan stood and addressed the assembly.

"Brothers, this is a sad day for Netzereth. Our beloved Rabbi, my mentor, and friend, Isaiah, is no longer among us." Matthan reached out his hand to steady himself on a wooden post that was nearby. His knees shook and it was obvious he was struggling to form his words. "The Sabbath was Rabbi Isaiah Ben Josiah's favorite day. It was his day to glory in the

Almighty and to serve all of us as he taught us the precepts of the One. To honor our beloved Rabbi, I have asked that the prescribed reading from the Prophets be changed to one of his favorite texts. We all know that he loved his namesake, the prophet Isaiah. It is in Isaiah that we understand the role of the Netzer and that we have become by heritage and choice the people of the Netzer, Netzerim. The Prophet Isaiah teaches us many things that we endeavor to follow with all our hearts. But the passage which our Rabbi Isaiah most enjoyed comes from another passage in Isaiah which I have asked to be read today."

At this, Judas stood up and approached the bema. He took the scroll of Isaiah from the ark and rolled it to the correct passage.

Judas read. "To me this is like the days of Noah, when I swore that the waters of Noah would never again cover the earth. So now I have sworn not to be angry with you, never to rebuke you again. Though the mountains be shaken and the hills be removed, yet my unfailing love for you will not be shaken nor my covenant of peace be removed, says the LORD who has compassion on you. O afflicted city, lashed by storms and not comforted, I will build you with stones of turquoise, your foundations with sapphires. I will make your battlements of rubies, your gates of sparkling jewels, and all your walls of precious stones. All your sons will be taught by the LORD, and great will be your children's peace. In righteousness you will be established: tyranny will be far from you; you will have nothing to fear. Terror will be far removed;

it will not come near you. If anyone does attack you, it will not be my doing; whoever attacks you will surrender to you."

Judas solemnly rolled up the scroll and added the blessing that came at the end of every public reading of the Torah, Prophets, or Writings. "To the Name and to His Netzer."

Matthan stood as Judas left the bema and said, "That is the peace toward which Isaiah worked his whole life. It is a peace promised to us through the Netzer whom we anxiously await. Isaiah worked to prepare the way for the Netzer. And he worked tirelessly to safeguard us from those who would wish to deceive us about the truth, because he wanted this peace which was promised by the Name, through His prophet, Isaiah. And now, with our beloved Rabbi dead, it is up to us to carry on his work."

Matthan continued on with his homily but James had lost interest. Instead his mind was racing down another path that had started with Matthan's claim that others wished to deceive the Netzerim about the truth. He understood the thinly veiled reference was to Jesus, but he had put a new spin on it. All along James believed that Jesus had left the ranks of the Netzerim and aligned himself with the Pharisees because he had been deceived. Jesus was following a path that led him away from the truth and the family prayed and worked for his return to the Netzerim. But Matthan's claim was upsettingly different. To Matthan, Jesus was the deceiver. Now the reference made a few days ago to Jesus being a monster, made sense. Could it be true that his brother who had always treated him with fairness, kindness, respect, and love was a deceiver? His teaching about the Almighty was so convincing, so convicting. Could he really have been working for the Evil One? Could someone who didn't seem to have a single flaw in his personality actually be the worst kind of person ever? Is it possible that he could have lived twenty-nine years with someone and be so wrong about him?

Suddenly James was roused from his own thoughts as the assembly stood in unison and began shouting. James stood and turned to his neighbor and asked what had happened.

"Matthan just announced that the trial of the murderous Jacob will take place first thing tomorrow morning and we will follow the law of Moses, not Roman law."

James felt the blood rush from his face and he sat back down on the bench with a thud. Matthan meant to have the Netzerim execute Jacob for the murder of Isaiah rather than hand him over to the Roman authorities.

Hadassah, Emma and the children walked back to James' house as quickly as possible. Emma cried the whole way with Jesse trying desperately to support and console his mother, and Hadassah followed carrying Sarah and cajoling Joshua to keep up as he pouted out of sympathetic fear for Emma.

Once inside the compound Emma turned suddenly and faced Hadassah. "I must go back to the synagogue and help my husband."

Hadassah hugged Emma as she tried to pass through the gate and held on as her friend broke down in uncontrollable sobs. "Emma, there is nothing you can do for him there. They will not let you see him. And he would worry all the more about you if he saw you like this. Let's sit and rest and get something for the children to eat. Perhaps we can even put something together for you to take to Jacob to eat this afternoon."

Hadassah led her friend to the table in the center of the courtyard and helped her sit on a bench.

"I just feel there must be something I can do to save my husband." Emma said through clenched teeth.

Hadassah wanted so badly to help her friend. She sat next to her and said "We can pray."

They held hands as they silently prayed to the Almighty for deliverance. After a few minutes Hadassah spoke out loud what she knew they both were feeling. "God of Abraham, Isaac, and Jacob, You protected your people through plague, flood, famine, captivity, and fire. Protect your servant Jacob now in his greatest need."

After a few more quiet moments Emma whispered, "Thank you Hadassah."

Hadassah pulled Emma's forehead to her and gave it a kiss. "I love you Emma. You are like a sister to me. And I will do whatever I can to help you and Jacob."

"Maybe there is something we can do." Emma's eyes lit up and she stood to her feet and ran to the stairway that led to the roof of Hadassah's room.

Hadassah followed as quickly as she could. "What are you...Where are you going?"

Jesse, carrying Sarah, and Joshua followed their mothers to the roof and soon all five of them were looking out over the Jezreel Valley to the Samaritan Mountains rising in the distance.

"What are we looking at Emma?"

"I lift up my eyes to the hills—where does my help come from? My help comes from the LORD the Maker of heaven and earth."

Hadassah recognized the Psalm as the one James and she had recited on their trips to Jerusalem to worship at the Temple. But she was still confused. "What are you talking about?"

"Your father lives in Nain doesn't he?" Emma asked.

"Yes he does but I still do not follow what you are talking about. Emma, are you okay? Maybe we should go back down and you should lay down for a bit."

"No, listen to me Hadassah. You are right, there is little I can do to save my husband, but there is someone who can. Jesus." She almost screamed the name in excitement.

"But he is in Jerusalem. And honestly he could make things worse..."

Emma interrupted, "All we need to do is go to Nain and ask your father to send a fast runner to Jerusalem to tell Jesus that his good friend Jacob needs help. He will come I am sure of it."

"But Emma, Nain is a day's walk from here and it is the Sabbath. And my children would never be able to make it. We wouldn't be able to get ten steps out of Netzereth before being stopped by someone and reminded of the Sabbath laws." Hadassah saw Emma's countenance fall as she threw up arguments against getting word to Jesus. So she stopped short of even explaining that by the time Jesus could get to Netzereth the trial would be over and Jacob possibly dead.

The two women stood side by side looking out over the valley, one in despair and the other sorry to have crushed her friends hope.

"I'll go mother."

The women suddenly realized that Jesse was standing next to them and were startled by his words. And they both responded to him at the same time.

"No."

But then Emma brightened and said, "Yes." Then turning to Hadassah she added, "Think about it. We need Jesus here. We would be seen making a trip in the middle of the Sabbath to Nain, but Jesse could hide in the fields and make much better time than we could. He could get to your father's home without being seen and ask for a runner to go to Jerusalem at the end of Sabbath. He has been to Nain many times with Jacob to sell cloth. He knows the way. Jesus could be here in four days."

"But it's too dangerous." Hadassah said pleading with her friend.

"Honestly Hadassah, I would rather that Jesse be safely out of Netzereth than here to see what will happen to his father."

"I'm going." Jesse looked at Hadassah with eyes of determination that indicated she was fighting a losing battle.

How could she let this happen? It was against the law, but a delay of a day would mean the sure death of Jacob and maybe Emma. It was dangerous, but Jesse was almost a man and knew the way and might be safer away from Netzereth. James would not approve, but Jesus could and would save the day. And it was obvious that Jesse and Emma were determined to do this, her help could make the trip safer.

"Okay." She relented. "You can go out our gate that leads to our garden out back and down the side of the hill. Stay off the roads. Go through the fields and stay in the taller grains. Do you see that hill over there?" She pointed to the hill of Moreh to the South East of Netzereth. "Nain is just on this side of that hill. Let's go down to the courtyard and pack a bag of bread for your trip."

After arguing with Matthan and Jeremiah till the sun was at its peak, James finally convinced them that it would only be right for them to allow him to speak with Jacob. They were concerned that James might be planning to help Jacob escape and James had to swear by the Throne of the Almighty that all he would do is talk about the trial scheduled for the next day. And he also agreed to help disperse the other Jacob supporters who were hanging around the synagogue.

James walked into the storage room that had been repurposed as a jail cell to see Jacob on his knees praying. His friend looked concerned but peaceful and this was no surprise to James.

"James, it's so good to see a friendly face." Jacob rose as he spoke and put his hands on James' shoulders.

"I would have been here earlier my friend if it would have been possible. First of all, I want you to know that your family is safe. Emma and Jesse are under my protection. They are worried about you but they are safe."

"Thank you my friend. I know they will be well cared for. But I also worry that you may have put your family in danger by helping me."

"You let me worry about that. You have enough to be concerned about. We need to talk about this preposterous claim that you are responsible for Isaiah's death." James motioned to a bench against the wall, inviting Jacob to sit with him.

James continued. "I had left the synagogue before Isaiah collapsed. Could you please explain to me what happened?"

"I'm not exactly sure what happened. I was explaining to the assembly what I believe to be your brother's true motive for his actions last week in Jerusalem. That in reality there is no threat to Netzereth at all. When Isaiah came up beside me and in that jovial way he has to disarm you when he wants to correct you... You know what I mean, don't you?"

James nodded.

"He put his arm around me and started laughing and before I knew it, he was completely on me. I lowered him to the floor and he was dead."

"What happened next?"

"Everyone rushed to Isaiah's side and I was pushed away. Then Matthan stood, looked at me and said, 'What did you do?' I just stood there… speechless. I froze. I didn't know what to say or do…. It wasn't my fault, James, I didn't do anything to Isaiah. I loved that man."

"I know, my friend, I loved him too. But unfortunately it's looking bad for you. Matthan and most of the Elders are claiming that you did something to Isaiah when he leaned on you. And since he died right before the Sabbath, his body was quickly prepared for burial before sundown. Therefore no one who would desire to prove your innocence had a chance to examine Isaiah's body for wounds. So I must ask you, were you carrying any knives or other weapons on you at that time?"

"No, of course n…oh, they did take my leather pouch from me that contains my sewing kit when they arrested me. In the kit was a pair of scissors and two long sewing needles."

James nodded and quietly thought about what options they had.

"I'm sorry James; you should distance yourself and your family from me as soon as possible. This will not end well for me."

"Jacob, you know me better than that. I will not abandon a friend who is in trouble. We will figure something out. Before I leave I want you to give me a complete list of everything that was in your sewing kit. Maybe we can get it back before it becomes a problem for us. Maybe they don't know yet what is in it."

"Thank you for your help James. Can I ask another favor of you? Can you send someone to inform Jesus of my situation? He may come to my aid."

"I can try but he is in Jerusalem and your trial begins tomorrow. There is no way we can get word to him in time." Jacob slumped his shoulders in defeat. "But we will send a messenger as soon as possible."

Jacob nodded. And then with renewed energy he asked, "Did you notice anything strange about Isaiah before he died?"

"Yes I did." James responded. "He was definitely feeling ill as Matthan said. He was slow to move and seemed to be short of breath."

"And I noticed that he was pale, and he kept rubbing his left arm like it was sore. I had an uncle once who died suddenly but had been complaining of chest and arm pain in the hours before his death. We never knew what killed him but thought it had to be connected to the pain he was feeling."

"Maybe I can go to Sepphoris tonight after the Sabbath and seek out the doctor that is there to care for the Magistrate. I hear that the Greeks have developed new ideas about health that could explain Isaiah's death."

"I'm not sure involving Gentiles in this is a good idea, but I think we may be able to convince some of the Elders that I had nothing to do with Isaiah's death by pointing to his health. Do what you think is best, James."

James left the Synagogue with a list of the contents of Jacob's leather pouch and a few meager ideas on how to help Jacob in the trial. He had also spent a good deal of time with Jacob in prayer to the Almighty asking for His guidance and help.

CHAPTER 10

(Saturday Afternoon)

Judas returned to the synagogue after James had left his meeting with Jacob. Their paths did not cross so Judas had no idea of what they had discussed just minutes before. Judas wasn't there to speak with Jacob however, and he walked directly to the scriptorium.

The scriptorium was a small room connected to the assembly room by a small narrow passage that had a curtain as a door. The scriptorium was where all the Holy Scripture scrolls were kept and studied and copied. It was Judas' regular custom to return to the synagogue on Sabbath afternoons to read Scripture. But today he arrived earlier than usual as the morning's assembly had raised some questions in his mind about the meaning of the passage he had read for Matthan that morning.

Judas also knew that if he read silently rather than out loud, as was the custom when reading Scripture, he could read faster and with less possibility of distraction from others who might hear him. He found the scroll he was looking for, kissed it, and carried it to his favorite reading desk. The desk, although completely visible from inside the scriptorium, was out of sight of anyone who might look through the curtained doorway into the room. He unrolled the scroll to the same place he had earlier that morning and began re-reading the same passage in Isaiah.

The question which was tickling Judas' mind was concerning the peace that Matthan had said was as a result of what the Netzer would do. And yet the Netzer is not mentioned in the passage at all. It is the Almighty that guarantees this peace. It is part of the covenantal commitment that The Name entered into with the righteous of Israel. How did Matthan connect this with the Netzer?

He continued reading silently and noticed that this peace was extended to foreigners who also obeyed The Almighty. "Okay, I guess that agrees with Essene teaching, but they have to become part of the covenant first." he thought. But nowhere was there a mention of the Netzer.

Judas then rolled the scroll back to the passage before the reading of the morning, and there it was. Not the actual word "netzer", but a close synonym.

> *Who has believed our message and to whom has*
> *the arm of the LORD been revealed? He grew*
> *up before him like a tender shoot, and like a root*
> *out of dry ground. He had no beauty or majesty*

*to attract us to him, nothing in his appearance
that we should desire him.*

He continued reading, recognizing that this was one of the suffering servant passages. As Rabbi Isaiah stated, before he died, this passage referred to the role of the nation Israel in The Almighty's plan to bring peace. But the idea of the Netzer being connected to this was intriguing. If the passage is read as an individual being the suffering servant rather than the nation, as in fact the grammar literally showed, then perhaps the Netzer was different than a ruling king. In this passage the suffering servant is put to death, led like a lamb to the slaughter, assigned a grave with the wicked!

And then Judas read the words that stopped him cold.

*He poured out his life unto death, and was
numbered with the transgressors. For he bore
the sin of many, and made intercession for the
transgressors.*

That is what Jacob was trying to say about Jesus. He said Jesus was a lamb being slain for our protection. He was the lamb that takes away the sin of the world.

Judas rose to go talk with Jacob. Or at least see if the guard would allow him to speak with him. But a sound in the assembly room made him sit down again. Someone had slammed the front door shut and there were voices. One of the voices was definitely Matthan's. Judas slid on his reading bench closer to the wall and farther from view of the curtained doorway.

The curtain flew open and Judas could see a hand on the curtain, but no one entered.

"We're alone. We can talk here." Elder Jeremiah said.

"Okay, we have two arguments to use tomorrow to convict Jacob. The first is his obvious support of the heretic Jesus. That alone, if used wisely, will allow us to banish Jacob's family from Netzereth and maybe other followers as well. But also this fact gives motive for Jacob to kill Isaiah. We must build on this. I will testify to the fact that Isaiah was advocating the removal of all Jesus followers from Netzereth. I want you to do the same and we will get Heber and Nathaniel to also testify to that. We will say it was part of our discussion at Passover meal."

"That sounds fine Rabbi, but isn't it our goal to do more than convict just Jacob of murder?"

"Yes Jeremiah. I remember our agreement that Ezra also take the fall in this trial. But first things first. We have motive established for Jacob to kill Isaiah but how do we establish how he killed him? Once we figure that out we can weave the story so that Ezra is also responsible."

"Well, do we know how Isaiah died? I know he was sick and he collapsed on Jacob, could we say Jacob poisoned him in some way?"

"I don't think that would work because then we would have to explain how Jacob added poison to Isaiah's food somehow. And to tell you the truth, I'm afraid a poisoning might point more to me since I lived with Isaiah and have benefited from his death. We need to stay away from that idea."

There was a long pause in the conversation and Judas thought that perhaps the two men had moved out of the assembly room into one of the connected smaller rooms. Then Matthan asked, "I saw the men who took custody of Jacob take a leather pouch away from him. What was in that pouch?"

"I'm not sure. Probably just some tailoring tools. I've seen Jacob on occasion fixing a ripped tunic on the streets when people were just passing by."

"What if one of those tools was used to stab Isaiah?"

"But there would have been blood."

Matthan chuckled, and said "I saw blood. Didn't you? Let's go take a look at that leather pouch."

When he was sure they were gone, Judas left the synagogue without being seen, and went straight home. James would want to know what he had just heard.

Jesse stopped within eyesight of his ultimate destination, Nain. The six mile trip had gone without major incident. He first descended the hills of Netzereth using an animal trail which he and his friends often used when playing together. This kept him off the main road which would have been a risky route. He did not want to be seen by anyone who might question why he was walking so far from home on the

Sabbath. The trail was hidden from human eyes and it was steep in areas. But by the Almighty's help he made it to the plains of Esdraelon with only a small tear in his tunic.

The trek across the plain of Esdraelon to the outskirts of Nain was quick and easy as Jesse stayed in the fields of grain rather than following the paths around the grain fields. By this method he was able to stay hidden in the grain as well as keep a straight course from the hills of Netzereth to the hill on which Nain sat.

Now, as the sun was nearing the western horizon, Jesse was looking at the main entrance to Nain from the safety of a small grain wagon in a nearby field and waiting for an opportunity to enter without being seen. Every once in a while Jesse could see a man outside his home on the main street of Nain. He seemed to be busy trying to get his chickens rounded up and into his courtyard. Every time Jesse thought the job was done and started to make a run for the town the man would pop out again chasing another chicken.

This is ridiculous, Jesse thought to himself, his father needed help right away, and the way is being blocked by chickens.

Finally, it appeared to be safe to walk into the town. Jesse slowly came out from behind the wagon and walked towards the path that led into Nain. Once he was on the path he was committed to the action. He now had to have a plausible reason for walking on the Sabbath if anyone should ask. He kept an eye on the house with the chickens and even heard the birds scratching at the gate of the home as he walked by.

But in focusing his attention on the house to his right with the chickens, he missed the three men who were standing next to the door of another home on his left. Suddenly a large rough hand grabbed Jesse by the ear and spun him around.

"Boy, why are you breaking the Sabbath? Who are your parents? I don't recognize you!"

"Ow! My name is Joshua", Jesse lied. "My mother, Hadassah, sent me here to get my Grandfather's help.'

"Not on the Sabbath she didn't. I know Johanan. He would not bear the insolence of his daughter allowing her son to break the Sabbath." Then, still holding Jesse by the ear the man began to drag him away. "Come, I am an Elder here in Nain and we obey the Sabbath to keep it holy. You will go with me to the Synagogue where you will pray for forgiveness and after sunset I will send for your Grandfather."

Judas entered the homestead to find everyone in the courtyard talking at the same time. Only little Sarah was playing quietly in a pile of limestone dust. Everyone else was shouting or crying or trying to get someone's attention. Through the commotion Judas was able to discern that Hadassah had done something that upset James. James was yelling at Hadassah. Emma was sobbing while trying to get James to stop yelling. Joshua was tugging on Hadassah's clothes whining, "I want to go with Jesse." Simon and Joseph were off to the side talking loudly to each other about Zerah and her father, David.

When finally there was a brief calm in the storm, Judas stood on a stool and boomed, "I have important news." Everyone turned and looked at Judas. For a moment the only noise was that of Sarah giggling in the dust.

"I overheard Matthan and Jeremiah plotting to frame Jacob and Ezra for the death of Isaiah and then banishing all Jesus followers from Netzereth." Emma ran to the great room wailing, Hadassah followed and on the way picked up Sarah. Joshua took one look at his father's face and quickly ran after his mother.

James looked up at Judas, moved to the meal table, and grumbled, "Let's talk."

The four brothers sat at the table and Judas asked, "What was all this arguing about?"

James sighed, and said "Hadassah and Emma sent Jesse to Nain hoping that Johanan could send someone to Jerusalem to get Jesus. And Joseph found out this morning that David wants to cancel the marriage contract."

"He doesn't want his daughter connected to the house of Jesus." Joseph spat.

"What did you hear?" James asked.

"I was in the Scriptorium when Elder Jeremiah and Rabbi Matthan came into the Synagogue. They are planning to use the sewing kit that Jacob always keeps on him to prove that he stabbed Isaiah. And then they are going to implicate

Elder Ezra as well. They have false witnesses lined up to support their claim."

"What? Who? This is so wrong. I'm telling you brothers, this is a very dangerous situation. We need to start carrying swords in our own village." Simon exclaimed.

Ignoring Simon, James focused his eyes on Judas and asked, "Do you know who the witnesses are?"

"I believe they are the rest of "The Leftovers", Heber and Nathaniel. Heber is attached to Matthan at the hip and Nathaniel is easily riled up by threats of Roman involvement. I don't think it will be of any use talking to them before the trial to get them to change their statements. What do you three think?"

Simon responded quickly, "We need to seize the time we have and act quickly to break Jacob out of his confinement. If we do it quickly and quietly we can save him and get out of this miserable town."

Joseph jumped in immediately. "No we can't leave Netzereth. I still intend to marry Zerah. We need to stay and change David's mind."

"We have to at least warn Ezra and Jacob of what is being planned against them. But, yes, Heber and Nathaniel are not going to go against Matthan" James said. "In my visit with Jacob today we came to the same conclusion that they would use his sewing kit against him. There are scissors and needles in the kit. I was going to try to get that kit before they knew what they had." James paused and shook his bowed head in thought. "It seems that Simon's plan is becoming our only option."

"But James."

"Joseph, you have one last chance to convince Zerah to leave with us. But we need to get Jacob out of that synagogue and get to safety. We will go to Sepphoris." Judas saw the alarm rise in Simon's face as James continued. "Perhaps we can get the leadership I have been doing work for there, to protect us. And I want to talk to the Greek doctor there about what killed Isaiah." Then looking at all three of his brothers with an intense stare he added. "This is a temporary measure. We have not given up on Netzereth or the rest of our friends here. We will be back."

CHAPTER 11

(Saturday Evening)

Johanan looked at the young boy asleep on the bench in the synagogue. He was much older than five year old Joshua, so that brought some relief to his heart knowing that his grandson hadn't hiked six miles across open country by himself. But he had no idea who this child was or why he said he was the son of Hadassah. This was a mystery, but it was also important. No one allows a child to break the Sabbath laws without a dreadful reason. He sat next to Jesse and shook him gently. "Wake up child."

Jesse sat up quickly and scooted away from the stranger.

"It's okay son. I am Hadassah's father. If you have come all the way from Netzereth alone on the Sabbath, it must be some very important news you bring. Is my daughter and her family okay?"

"Yes. No. I mean, I don't know. I...I..."

Johanan reached out and touched Jesse on the shoulder to calm him. "Relax boy. First tell me who you are."

"My name is Jesse Ben Jacob of Netzereth."

"Do you know my daughter's family?" Jesse nodded his head and began to whimper. Johanan slid next to Jesse and whispered, "Why don't you tell me what is happening in Netzereth."

"Emma, would it be possible to speak with you?" Judas spoke through the door of the great room after knocking.

From inside, Emma answered. "Just a moment, Judas. I'm coming out. Are we ready to go?"

The brothers had spent the last few hours talking through a plan to get the family safely out of Netzereth and rescue Jacob from his imprisonment. Emma was in complete agreement with the plan. She was looking forward to being with Jacob again, although she knew it was risky. Currently everyone was readying themselves for the night's activities. Joseph had quickly packed a bag and then left to speak with David about Zerah one last time. James and Hadassah were packing the family donkey for a long walk to Sepphoris. Simon was getting knives and swords together for the jailbreak they had planned. James made it clear that no one was to be injured but agreed that they had to have a show of force.

"No, we want to wait for a bit more darkness before leaving." Judas responded through the door. "I wanted to talk to you about something Jacob said at the town council before Isaiah died."

Emma opened the door and stepped outside curious as to what Judas might be thinking. "I wasn't there Judas. I don't know what he said."

"You might. He was talking about Jesus being called by John the baptizer, 'the Lamb which takes away the sin of the world.'"

"Oh, yes, that was an idea which came upon him while we ate our Passover meal. Jesse had drawn a connection between the Passover Lamb and the way Jesus had responded to the crowds who wanted to make him king of Israel. Jacob and I then began thinking that Jesus wasn't the Netzer in the way so many of us had thought him to be. Instead of ruling a kingdom he was sacrificing himself to usher in a new relationship with the Almighty. So, Jacob thought if he could convince the Elders of this thinking they would recognize that we need not fear Rome's armies here in Netzereth."

"I think he may have been on to something." Judas responded. "I was reading a passage in the Prophet Isaiah this afternoon that has always been seen as speaking of the Nation Israel as The Almighty's suffering servant. I think it is possible to read it as the Netzer being The Almighty's suffering servant. I need to do some more study on this, but this may change the way we all view the Netzer. After we rescue Jacob tonight I want to sit down and talk about everything you two know about my brother's ministry."

Judas had a gleam in his eyes as he turned and walked away from Emma. She was familiar with that look. It was the response many people had when they began to understand

and track with Jesus' teachings. She looked forward to some long conversations with Judas and Jacob. The thought of being with Jacob by the end of the night, filled her with joy.

Jesse and Johanan walked the streets of Nain on their way to Johanan's home. Jesse had explained as best he could the situation in Netzereth and Johanan had listened thoughtfully.

"I'm glad you are willing to help. I'm afraid I might not see my father again." Jesse said with his head bowed as he walked.

"Have you ever had any interaction with Jesus, son?" Johanan responded.

Jesse's head rose and his eyes lit up as he shared with his new friend the experience he had in sharing his lunch with Jesus and a large crowd of people. After hearing the story, Johanan said, "I was in that crowd. I went to hear what Jesus had to say. His teaching about the Kingdom of God was amazing. And then we were told to sit in groups of fifty so that food could be shared with us. I didn't know it was your lunch." Johanan smiled down at Jesse. "It didn't make any sense to me. Who would have brought enough food to feed all of us out there? Then two of his disciples walked by on either side of the group and handed us some bread and fish. And it kept coming. So I asked one of the disciples where all the food was coming from. And he shared that he was just as confused as all of us. Our group of fifty began talking about how it was near Passover and how the Almighty provided manna and quail every day in the wilderness. The connection was obvious to us all. Jesus was the prophet Moses had promised would come. Jesus was the Messiah. And with his knowledge of the Kingdom of Heaven, he had to be our king. But then…, he just disappeared. To this day I have wondered why he doesn't claim the throne of David."

"My father thinks he is here to die."

Jesse's words stopped Johanan in his tracks. Then he shook his head and continued his stride. "You are just a child. You don't understand. Your father meant something else I'm sure. But either way, here we are at my home. And since you fed me your lunch on that remarkable day two years ago, I will now feed you dinner as we decide what must be done for our families in Netzereth."

Johanan opened the gate to his courtyard and both he and Jesse entered. Jesse saw at the center of the courtyard a table with eight people seated around it. Everyone stood as Johanan approached and the questions started flying. Jesse tried to hide behind Johanan's robes as the master of the house settled everyone down. Johanan introduced Jesse and asked him to sit on his left. The rest of the household made room for the newcomer and introductions were made. Johanan took the lead in sharing the story of why Jesse was in Nain. Jesse began to feel at ease and added details as the others asked for clarification. All the while everyone enjoyed a wonderful meal of chicken, grape salad, and warm bread.

Seated to the left of Jesse was Caleb, the eldest son of Johanan, Hadassah's brother. It was decided that he would go to Jerusalem the fastest way possible, through Samaria. He would take the family donkey so as to rest while still moving. With the blessing of the Almighty, it would take him a full day to make the trip. It was decided that he would begin within the hour as travel by night, although dangerous because of thieves and darkness, was faster because of cool weather and no Roman patrols.

Jesse begged to go along with Caleb. He argued that he knew Jesus. That Jesus would believe him. That it was his father who was in trouble and needed him. But all his arguments were shot down by Johanan who argued that Caleb could move faster without Jesse along and the trip was much too dangerous for a child to make. Eventually Jesse saw his arguments were falling on deaf ears and gave up. He watched as Caleb packed a few supplies, bridled the donkey, and started out on the path that led south to Jerusalem. Jesse said a prayer of protection for Caleb and his father and then went to a corner of the courtyard where Johanan's family had set a bed for him for the night. He lay down and silently wept for his father.

Joseph had returned from the home of David with a wild look on his face. David had still refused to honor the marriage contract between Joseph and Zerah but Joseph had a new plan. He pulled James to the side and made his offer.

"You want to make sure your family gets to Sepphoris safely. Emma wants to make sure Jacob is rescued successfully. You will need Simon's ability with weapons and Judas' knowledge of the synagogue and those who work there in order to get Jacob out. I am the logical choice to safely get your family out of Netzereth. And I am even willing to take them to Sepphoris if I can take Zerah as well."

"You do not want to do that Joseph. How can you think of involving Zerah in this against her father's wishes? You would bring down even more condemnation upon us. No, you can not do this."

"Well then James, I stay here. David has said that he will reinstate the marriage contract if I disown my family and especially Jesus. I will stay in Netzereth. I will find land to build a place for Zerah. I am willing to work extra hard to win her to me again. I would prefer to keep my brothers as well as my wife but if you are making me choose…"

James hung his head in thought and frustration. Joseph had correctly assessed the situation and knew that James needed him to get his family to safety. And it was David who was breaking faith with the marriage contract. But why another stumbling block in the road to keeping this family together? Why had Jesus placed such a heavy burden on him?

"Fine" James finally answered. "But you must keep David in the dark about this until all of us are safely away from this place."

Joseph jumped with excitement. "No problem, Zerah has already agreed to sneak away from her home and meet us on the road to Sepphoris. David will be clueless until tomorrow morning. By then we will all be in Sepphoris."

Joseph turned and quickly walked to where the women and children were waiting. He threw his small pack on the back of the donkey and took the bridle in his hands.

James approached Hadassah and his children. "I love you all. I will see you in Sepphoris." And turning to Emma he said, "And I'll bring you your husband."

Emma smiled at him and whispered, "Thank you."

Hadassah looked at James with tearful eyes. "Be careful husband."

James hugged her and the sleeping Sarah in her arms. He then reached down and picked up Joshua, placing him on the donkey. "Be good son. And obey your uncle and mother."

They all walked to the courtyard gate and quietly opened it. James peered out and then nodded that all was clear. His family, the people he loved most, walked out into the darkness. James closed the gate behind them and prayed for their safety.

Caleb had made good time and covered a lot of ground in the two hours since leaving Nain. The path was a narrow trail that led up into the Samaritan hill country. He had traveled under the cover of darkness around the western edge of Mt. Gilboa and was approaching the small village of En-Gannim. If the rest of the trip went as smoothly as this first part, he would be in Jerusalem talking with Jesus by tomorrow afternoon.

"*What was that?*" he thought, as he turned around to search the darkness behind him. Something was on the path behind him, approaching him quickly. Caleb quickened his pace and reached a slight bend in the path. He pulled the donkey around the bend and then behind a large mustard bush. He waited as the noise got louder. It was obviously someone running on the path. Then the shape of a young lad ran past where Caleb was hiding.

"Jesse."

Jesse stopped, turned around to look at Caleb and trotted back to him. "Good I caught you." he panted. "I'm coming with you."

"Jesse, this is foolishness. You should not be out here alone. You should not be out here at all."

"But I am. And I'm going with you to Jerusalem. I need to get Jesus to help my father. He will listen to me. We are friends."

"You are just a child. Men of Jesus' stature don't listen to children. Oh what am I going to do with you now?"

Jesse stood tall as he had finally caught his breath. "The only thing you can do now. Take me with you."

Jesse stared at Caleb and Caleb shook his head as he said, "Well let's get going. We are losing time standing here." They began walking down the path in silence until Caleb finally said, "You know, you are not the only one who has a relationship with Jesus. Jesus and I have known each other for over 7 years now. I first met him when he came to ask my father to enter a marriage contract with him for James and Hadassah. He came back a few more times to visit our home and check on Hadassah while James prepared a place for her in Netzereth. We became friendly."

Jesse walked along silently. Caleb had to silence a chuckle as he recognized a bit of himself in this young lad. This boy had built up a relationship with Jesus because he had shared his lunch and was from the same town. Yes, his father and Jesus were friends. But Caleb also had a friendship with Jesus. Perhaps Jesse needed to hear that this wasn't just Jesse's mission to seek help from a friend. It was also his own.

"Keep up Jesse, you are walking too slow." Caleb called from ten feet ahead. Jesse sped up to catch up.

"Do you remember my wife Deborah? She was seated at the other end of the table from us."

"Yes, I think so. She was wearing the white head scarf, right?"

"Yes she's the one. We were married last year. She is the only daughter of a widow in our town and she has one brother, Seth. Her brother was the only one who was providing for the family and he became ill. After two months of doctors and the prayers of neighbors, Seth succumbed to the illness and died. Deborah and her mother were alone. She was not yet of marrying age and there was no other family to care for them. They had a small home to live in but Deborah's mother had no skills other than growing things in their small garden. She seriously considered selling herself and Deborah as slaves to a Roman soldier who had been searching recently for a housekeeper and stable boy."

"That would have been an awful life. I've seen how the Romans treat their slaves." Jesse responded. "Obviously she isn't a slave. What happened?"

"Jesus happened." As we were carrying the body of Seth, Deborah's brother, out to the tombs, Jesus arrived. He had a large number of people gathered around him asking questions and wanting his attention. When he saw us he set aside everything that was going on around him and walked up to Deborah's mother. He whispered some words to her and wiped away her tears with his tunic. He then told us to put the body of Seth down. He spoke just a few words to Seth. 'Young man, I say to you, get up.'" Caleb had to swallow some tears of his own as he shared the next few sentences. "Deborah has her brother back. Two people were saved from a life of slavery. And I have a beautiful wife. All because Jesus stepped into my life." Caleb paused for a minute to allow the truth to sink in for Jesse.

"Jesse, I know you have a special relationship with Jesus, but so do other people. Jesus is a remarkable man and hopefully our king someday. And I know this mission to speak to Jesus is important to your family. But sometimes you need to trust that others know what is best and allow them to help you. You are very brave to do this for your family but you are also foolish for not allowing others to help you."

Jesse looked at Caleb and nodded. "Thank you Caleb. I will trust you to get us to Jesus quickly and safely. And I'm sorry if I have messed things up."

"Don't worry about it friend. But let's pick up the pace a bit. We can make better time."

James, Judas, and Simon stood, in the dark, twenty yards away from the door of the synagogue. There was one man sitting on a bench under the half-constructed porch. As James looked at it, realizing the final column was still in his courtyard, it gave him that feeling of unfinished business which he hated. And his gut became even more twisted as he realized that what they were about to do would create even more unfinished work, relationships, and situations. But this had to be done. He had made promises. Jacob needed to be rescued from a corrupt system and corrupt men.

"Do you think there are more guards inside, Judas?" Simon said interrupting James' thoughts.

"Hard to say. There shouldn't be at this time of night."

The streets of Netzereth had been empty for over an hour. All the lamps were out in every home and the men had arrived at the synagogue only by the light of the slim new moon.

"How should we do this?" James whispered. "We can't surprise him since he is sitting with his back to the wall."

"We get his back off the wall." Simon responded. "I'll go around to the far side of the building and make a noise that will get him up to investigate. When he turns his back to you, you both grab him making sure to cover his mouth so he doesn't sound an alarm. Then we gag him and tie him up inside the Synagogue where someone can release him tomorrow."

"Sounds like you've done this before." Judas quipped

"Okay, let's do it. But remember, no knives unless absolutely necessary. And we don't know if anyone is inside other than Jacob so be alert." James instructed the brothers as Simon slipped away.

It wasn't more than a minute before James and Judas saw the guard's head turn away and then the man rise from the bench and move to the far corner of the porch. They quickly and quietly ran to the synagogue and reached the guard just as he turned the corner. James threw a sash over the guard's head and covered his mouth with his hands. The man struggled and tried to reach for a short sword he had at his waist. But Simon was right there to take the sword from him and Judas grabbed both wrists and wrestled them up behind the man's back causing him to surrender to his assailants.

"We don't wish to hurt you friend." James whispered in his ear. "Don't struggle, and you will be safe. We only want to rescue Jacob. You will not be harmed."

Within minutes the brothers had entered the synagogue, tied up the guard, and found Jacob sleeping in a barred room. They lifted the bar and woke Jacob with a gentle shake.

"Get up Jacob; we're getting you out of here." James smiled as he thought of the joy he would have at reuniting Jacob with his wife in Sepphoris.

Jacob woke slowly and looked around the room. "James... Simon... Judas, wh...what are you doing here?'

"We're here to rescue you, brother. Now get up we need to get moving." Simon responded.

James had begun to stuff Jacob's possessions in a bag when he was caught off guard by Jacob's next words.

"I don't want to be rescued. I want to stand trial tomorrow."

All three brothers stared at Jacob.

"You don't understand, we are here to take you to your wife and son who need you. Judas has information about the trial. It is all a scheme to get rid of the Jesus followers. You are in danger of losing your life friend. You must come with us. It is your only hope." James was pulling at Jacob as he spoke and Jacob in response was defiantly resisting.

Judas sat next to Jacob, "Friend your life is in danger. I know that Rabbi Matthan and Elder Jeremiah are scheming to convict you of the murder of Isaiah. They have even arranged for false witnesses to testify against you. You must come with us."

"Friends," Jacob searched the brothers' eyes as he spoke, "I believe Jesus is the Netzer. He is the Messiah. But most of all he is the Lamb who has come to take away the sin of the world. And although I do not understand everything that entails, I do know this. Everyone needs to know who Jesus is. When he lived here in Netzereth I knew him as the Netzer and he taught me what obedience to The One means. When I followed him with the crowds I knew him as the Messiah and he taught me how to live in the kingdom of the

Almighty. And in this last week I have come to know him as the Lamb and he has been teaching me what it means to sacrifice for others."

"What do you mean he has been teaching you this past week? He isn't here. He's in Jerusalem announcing his kingship."

"No James, he's here." Jacob placed his hand on his forehead. "All this week he has been teaching me by reminding me of what he taught while here in Netzereth and out in the countryside. His words are in me and he is calling me to obedience. He wants me to tell others who he is. My trial tomorrow isn't for the murder of Isaiah. My trial tomorrow is whether or not I will submit to my king and tell those around me that his kingdom is not of this world but rather the kingdom of heaven where our sin is forgiven by the sacrifice of the Lamb."

Jacob looked at all three men with a calm assurance of what he had just said. And they looked at him in disbelief.

After about a minute of stunned silence. James asked, "Do you remember last week when I came to you and asked if Jesus was a monster? It was right after we heard of Jesus' entry into Jerusalem as crowds shouted for his kingship. Do you remember what you told me?"

"Yes, I said that we don't have all the information yet."

"You reminded me of my brother's love for me and the family. And we don't have all the information yet. Are you telling me now that the Almighty wants you to walk into what is surely a deadly situation even though we lack vital information?"

"James, we do not have all the information yet about what Jesus is doing in Jerusalem, but we do have enough information to obediently follow the Almighty and lift up the name of His Netzer. I am convinced that this is my task tomorrow. Yes, I am fearful of the men who wish to destroy me but that will not keep me from doing what is right. I am following in the footsteps of our forefathers, who obeyed The Holy One even when they didn't understand why. Moses led the people into a trap at the Red Sea and obediently stretched out his rod over the sea not knowing why he was commanded to do so. Joshua led the people around Jericho with trumpets because he trusted The Almighty. Hananiah, Mishael, and Azariah refused to worship the king's image in order to obey The Name, not knowing they would be saved from the fiery furnace."

"Jacob, I wish I had your confidence that this is the right decision."

"My friends," Jacob looked each of the brothers in their eyes, "ask The One for wisdom. He will generously give it to all who ask sincerely. I know I must share with Netzereth who Jesus is."

Simon turned away from Jacob and stepped to the door to check on the guard. "What are we doing James? We have a captive out there who could eventually free himself and a captive in here who doesn't want to be freed."

James looked at Jacob who smiled back. "Thanks for the concern James, but I'm in the Almighty's hands. Right where I want to be."

"What am I supposed to tell your wife? She is expecting us to show up with you in Sepphoris in the morning?"

"Tell her the same thing. I'm in the Almighty's hands. Right where I want to be." Jacob looked James unblinkingly in the eyes and James knew he could not change Jacob's mind. "Oh, and tell her I love her and Jesse very much." Jacob added with a big grin.

James sighed and turned to his brothers, "Let's go." And then turning to Jacob he said, "I hope you know what you are doing."

The three brothers shut Jacob in his room and put the bar back on the door. They then made sure the guard was tied tightly and left the synagogue defeated and confused.

CHAPTER 12

(Sunday Morning)

James spent five minutes in a heated discussion with David about the disappearance of Zerah and Joseph before entering the synagogue. David was threatening to approach the elders with evidence of James' family kidnapping his daughter. It was issue that would have to wait till after the trial.

The synagogue was filled to the corners, no standing room at all. In fact women and children were not only in the balcony but also out on the porch. The trial of Jacob was the most important thing that had happened to Netzereth since the arrival of Joseph and Mary from their exile in Egypt. The difference between the two events was not lost on James as he surveyed the crowd. He was told that the whole town welcomed the couple and the baby with open arms and shouts of joy. The crowd today was not at all unanimous in their support of the Netzer. The majority were solidly in Matthan's camp calling for the death of the murderer of their beloved teacher Isaiah. But James was impressed with the turnout of those who supported Jacob and by extension Jesus. It seemed to James that the secret followers of Jesus were no longer secret.

There was a rumor being passed around about some escape attempt during the night which had been foiled by the guard on duty. The guard claimed that he had drawn his sword and the rescuers had run for their lives. A search was on for the six men who had attacked him but as he was not able to identify any of them, no arrests had been made.

The ten elders of Netzereth were sitting on the bema awaiting the arrival of Matthan and Jacob. Ezra was sitting with them but was clearly uncomfortable. Judas had been able to get word to him about the plans he had overheard the day before. James had thought that with the tide turning against him, Ezra would have avoided this trial. But he was encouraged to see Ezra up there. Perhaps he had spoken with the other elders and convinced them of the sham this trial was going to be.

Jeremiah was also on the bema with the other elders. And he looked nervous as well. He kept looking over the crowd as if someone he was expecting to be there was missing. Maybe their plan to convict Jacob and implicate Ezra was falling apart. James could only hope.

His brothers, Judas and Simon, stood next to him on the left side of the room as they had arrived too late to get a bench seat. They were silent, but alert to what was happening as the room of men slowly moved and flowed with each new piece of gossip that was being passed around. James silently prayed to the Almighty for deliverance.

A hush came over the crowd as Matthan emerged from the scriptorium to the right of the assembly room and ascended the steps of the bema. He stood in the middle and faced the crowd. "Men of Netzereth, I thank you all for joining us for this important day of justice. Just two days ago our Teacher, our Mentor, our Friend was tragically taken from us. Today we will seek justice for the life of Isaiah, a great man of faith."

"Laying the praise on a little thick, wouldn't you say?" Simon whispered in James' ear. James nodded.

"Our brother Jeremiah," Matthan continued, "will be acting as 'Head of the Sitting' for this proceeding as I will be called on as a witness against the accused. But before I turn the Head of the Sitting role over to him, I would just like to say that I am pleased to see the whole town of Netzereth has turned out for these proceedings. It speaks of how much love we all have for Isaiah." Matthan stepped to the side of the bema as a murmur of ascent to his words rumbled through the crowd.

Jeremiah stood and stepped up to the front of the bema with his arms raised to signal for silence. "Men of Netzereth, as you know, in matters judicial we must convene a Lesser Sanhedrin. But since we are a small town of only 10 sitting Elders and one Rabbi, we have had to ordain 13 more men to sit on this Lesser Sanhedrin. I ask those men to come and take their places in the Lesser Sanhedrin."

Immediately 13 men stood from various places in the assembly room and took seats in the semi-circle at the back of the bema. James couldn't help but notice that Matthan kept his seat in the Lesser Sanhedrin. He also recognized that all the new judges were outspoken in their distain of Jesus.

Once everyone was seated, Jeremiah began again. "We will begin by bringing out the man who has been accused of killing Isaiah, our beloved Rabbi."

The storage room behind the congregation where Jacob was being held was opened and out stepped Jacob, escorted by two guards. One of whom was the guard that was so easily overpowered the night before and now had the reputation of a mighty swordsman. The crowd parted as the three approached the bema and stopped short of ascending the steps. They faced Jeremiah in the middle of the Lesser Sanhedrin.

Jeremiah continued, "Jacob you have been accused of killing Isaiah our Rabbi on the sixth day, just hours before the beginning of Sabbath, right here in this very room. There were many witnesses to this act and we are bringing a few of them forward today to testify as to what they saw. You will silently listen to their testimony and then you will be given a chance to offer a defense for what you did. Do you understand?"

Jacob nodded and whispered something that James was not able to catch but Jeremiah seemed to understand and nodded in return.

"I call as first witness, Matthan." Jeremiah announced.

Matthan stood and walked to the top step of the bema. Jeremiah took his seat in the center of the semi-circle of chairs of the Lesser Sanhedrin and began the questioning.

"Matthan, please tell us what you witnessed this past sixth day while Jacob was speaking."

"We were gathered to discuss what we as the Netzer Community should do concerning the coming retribution of the gentiles for the obvious visual claim to the throne by the imposter Jesus. Isaiah had graciously allowed Jacob to speak as he had informed us that he had an important insight into the role of the Netzer. However as he spoke he put forward a ridiculous, heretical theory which Isaiah felt needed to be immediately addressed as it was sowing discord and confusion in the community. Isaiah, in his affable way, approached Jacob, and politely asked him to stop spreading lies about the Netzer. At that point Isaiah collapsed on top of Jacob who in turn thrust a pair of scissors into the chest of Isaiah. I quickly ran to Isaiah's aid and put my hand on his chest to stop the bleeding. And I also put my ear to his heart only to hear that it had stopped. The attack was swift and effective." Matthan then looked directly at Jacob as he said, "Jacob killed Isaiah."

The room erupted with shouts from all sides. The supporters of Jacob screamed their disapproval and accused Matthan of lying to the Lesser Sanhedrin. The supporters of Matthan cried in anguish as they relived the memory of the day and verbally attacked those who were disrupting the testimony of their Rabbi. Even James, Judas, and Simon were caught up in the emotional outbursts.

But then James caught sight of Jacob. He was standing perfectly still, looking straight into the face of his accuser. He was the epitome of peace. This sight brought wonder and peace to James. His thoughts turned to his older brother who always seemed to be in control of his emotions when being brought to task by someone. Jesus never responded with anger or contempt when someone accused him of wrong doing. He always had that same look that Jacob had right now. A patient, controlled, peace that demonstrated respect but also reserved the right to disagree.

James' eyes moved to Matthan who was surveying the crowd in the room with a hint of a smile. He thinks he has scored a blow in his deceit, thought James. And then James saw Matthan's gaze rest on Jacob, and the hint became a full fledged grin.

In seconds Jeremiah was up calling the room to order. He warned that men who could not control themselves would be required to leave and even motioned the two guards next to Jacob to turn and face the crowd. After a quick minute the crowd settled down and Jeremiah returned to his seat in the Lesser Sanhedrin and Matthan turned to face the judges once again.

Jeremiah asked, "You actually saw Jacob thrust the scissors into Isaiah's chest?"

"Well, no. I was at their backs when the deed was done but as soon as I got to Isaiah's side I saw the scissors in Isaiah and Jacob still bending over him."

"Did you touch the scissors?"

"Yes. I pushed Jacob aside and removed the scissors and tried to stop the bleeding. I then put my ear to his chest and knew there was no hope."

Jeremiah continued after a moment of silence, "What did you do next?"

"I yelled out that Jacob had killed our Rabbi and ordered some men nearby to hold Jacob. I then had some others help me carry the body of our Rabbi out of the synagogue to his home."

"Who were the men who held Jacob?"

"I believe they were Josiah, Hazael, and Tomas."

"And who helped you with Isaiah's body?"

"That would be Heber, and Jonas." Matthan responded.

"What happened next?"

"At Isaiah's home, Heber and I began preparing the body for burial as the Sabbath was quickly approaching. It was at that time that the sky went dark. I sent Jonas back to the synagogue to inform you to take whatever measures you deemed necessary with the meeting, the strange darkness, and the murderer." As Matthan said these last words he turned to look at Jacob with a look of derision. He then turned back to Jeremiah and added, "I am sorry that I had to put you in such a position but I knew you could handle it and I was overcome with grief for my mentor and friend. I heard that you did an outstanding job of leading the people in prayers of sorrow for our beloved Rabbi and safety from evil." At this a number of murmurs of ascent rippled through the crowd and Jeremiah brightened at the praise.

"Thank you Matthan. It was a difficult day for all of us. I was only doing what the Almighty ordained me to do in caring for our community."

James recognized something peculiar in the way Jeremiah responded. It was rehearsed, unusual words for Jeremiah to say. James immediately saw this was a scripted trial.

"One final question I have for you. What would motivate Jacob to commit such a heinous act?"

"I'm not sure, but perhaps he had heard that Isaiah was considering banishing the heretic's followers from Netzereth as a sign to the Gentile authorities that we did not support Jesus' claim to the thrown of David. Jacob was the most outspoken believer in Jesus' claims. And the threat of excommunication from the Netzerim was probably too much for him."

"Thank you Rabbi. That is all the questions I have for you," Jeremiah continued. "Does anyone else on the Lesser Sanhedrin have any other questions for this witness?"

"I do." Ezra said. Matthan turned slightly to face Ezra. "You said you pulled the scissors out of Isaiah's chest. Do you know what happened to the scissors?"

"I do not. I placed them on this bema. That is the last I saw of them."

"You did not see any of the men you have mentioned pick them up? Josiah? Hazael? Tomas? Heber? Jonas?"

At the mention of each name Matthan shook his head. "No, I have no idea what happened to the scissors."

"One last question," Ezra added. "Why was Isaiah's body rushed away from here so quickly? I understand the need to prepare the body for burial before the Sabbath, but there seemed to be plenty of time to do that. It seems to me that you were overly zealous in your desire to remove the body from sight."

Matthan stood silent a second before responding. "I understand that looking back it may seem that I acted quickly. But I was sure of what had happened. Jacob had killed my mentor, our Rabbi. We had the murderer in custody, and my love for my teacher overwhelmed me. I moved quickly to save him the shame of death and to protect the congregation from having a gruesome sight be the last memory of our beloved Rabbi." Matthan touched his eyes as if wiping away tears.

"Thank you Matthan for your devotion to Isaiah and the people of Netzereth." Jeremiah stepped forward as he spoke. He patted Matthan on the back and gave him a look of sympathy and respect. "Please have a seat. I wish to call our next witness." Jeremiah looked over the crowd as Matthan returned to his seat. "Josiah, would you please approach the Lesser Sanhedrin and answer some questions about what you saw?"

Josiah ascended the steps of the bema and faced the Lesser Sanhedrin.

Jeremiah began his questioning. "Where were you in the Synagogue as Jacob was speaking about the crazy idea that the Netzer would be a suffering servant?"

"Was that just before Isaiah was attacked?" Josiah asked.

Jeremiah nodded in response and added, "Yes, I'm trying to get an idea of what your view of the attack was."

"I was standing in the front. The room was very full so I was without a seat. I stood right about there." Josiah pointed to a spot to the far right of the bema on the floor. "I didn't want to block the view of those sitting in the front row."

"Is Matthan correct that you held Jacob away from Isaiah's body?"

"Yes, I had jumped up on the bema when I saw Isaiah go down. I wanted to help him back up but Matthan was there first and he told me to grab Jacob."

Jeremiah leaned forward and asked, "Did you see Jacob stab Isaiah?"

"I saw Isaiah double over on Jacob and that must have been when the killer struck."

"And there we have the testimony of two witnesses who saw Jacob kill Isaiah" Jeremiah said with finality.

"I have a few questions." Ezra announced. "When you, Hazael, and Tomas were restraining Jacob did you notice if he was in possession of his sewing kit which he always keeps tied to his waist?"

"Yes it was there and when we escorted him to the storage room as the Elders asked, we took the kit from him and gave it to the Elders."

"Which elder in particular did you give the kit to?"

Josiah paused in thought and then said, "I believe it was Elder Joseph specifically but he was with a group of about four elders at the time."

After a short silence Jeremiah continued, "Thank you Josiah, you may be seated. I would now like to bring up Heber to share with us what he observed as he helped prepare Isaiah's body for burial."

Heber ascended the dais and faced the Lesser Sanhedrin. James was aware that this testimony in particular couldn't be trusted and so he listened carefully in order to catch some inconsistency which could be used to help Jacob.

"Heber, where were you when Isaiah was stabbed by Jacob?"

"I was sitting four benches back in the center of the room."

"And what did you witness?" Jeremiah continued.

"I saw Isaiah approach Jacob from the rear smiling and correcting his heretical words. It was classic Isaiah. He laughed and put an arm around Jacob and then corrected him. It then looked like he was about to hug Jacob but instead he collapsed at his feet. At that moment the whole assembly stood to rush to his aide and I was trapped in my place by the swarm of people wishing to help the Rabbi. It was then that Matthan called me up to the bema to help him remove the body of our beloved Rabbi." Heber paused to wipe his eyes and nose and began again with a feeble voice. "Matthan lifted Isaiah by his arms while Jonas and I carried his legs." At this, Heber hung his head and stopped speaking.

Jeremiah pressed on, "What happened next?"

Heber whispered, "We took him…"

"What? You must speak up Heber! The Lesser Sanhedrin needs to hear your testimony."

"We took him to his home and laid him on his bed. Matthan sent Jonas back to the synagogue and the two of us prepared his body for burial."

"Thank you, Heber. I know this is hard but can you tell us what you believe to be the cause of his death?"

Heber looked up and scanned the Lesser Sanhedrin. "There was a large wound on the left side of his chest. I believe that Jacob stabbed him with his scissors, stopping his heart."

"Thank you Heber. Are there any other questions for this witness?"

Ezra rose from his seat and approached Heber. "Why did Matthan call for you specifically, Heber, to come help him?

"You will have to ask him that to be sure but I assume it is because I was very close to Isaiah. We just had Passover meal with him we did many things together as friends and I was trained at the Wilderness School and was familiar with the rites and procedures necessary to prepare a body for burial."

"Thank you Heber. One last question. With a stab to the heart there should have been a large amount of blood. And yet as I look at this very bema where Isaiah died there is not even a stain of blood. Why is that?"

"Elder Ezra that is a very good question. And there are several reasons for that. First of all we removed Isaiah's body so quickly that no blood was able to get to the floor. Secondly, Isaiah wore his tunic wrapped very tightly around his waist and chest as he was aware that he was a big man and wished to hide how big he was. I believe his extra skin and weight also kept the wound from bleeding and it was only in preparing his body did most of his blood come out through the wound. There are ample blood stains on his bed and floor of his room."

Ezra furrowed his brow in thought but then nodded and returned to his seat.

James noticed something else. Heber seemed to be upset at losing a friend but when the talk of blood came up he seemed very calm and factual. "There's the lie." he thought to himself.

Jeremiah was ready to move on. He called Nathaniel up to the bema. As he ascended, Jeremiah announced, "This will be our last witness and then Jacob will have a chance to explain why he killed our Rabbi."

He continued as he addressed Nathaniel, "My first question is the same as I have asked others. Where were you sitting when the attack happened?"

I was right there on the front bench. I arrived early to the meeting in order to get a good seat. I have a vested interest in the issue of the Roman scum and their interference with our way of life."

"Yes we are all aware of your situation but please just answer the questions. I understand you have some specific information about what happened here. Tell us what you saw."

"I agree with all that has been said so far. But I can add that I saw Jacob pick up the scissors and place them back in his sewing kit before he was restrained by the three men."

A gasp rippled through the assembly and Jeremiah asked, "By the three men you mean Josiah, Hazael, and Tomas, correct?"

Nathaniel nodded his assent to the question and Jeremiah quickly turned to Elder Joseph. "Joseph, where did you put that sewing kit?"

Elder Joseph jumped up and left the room shouting, "I'll go get it."

Elder Ezra quickly stood and asked Nathaniel, "How is it that you alone saw what happened to the scissors?"

Nathaniel shrugged and responded, "I guess I was watching Jacob more than the others here. Everyone else was so concerned about Isaiah but I was concerned about the lies Jacob was saying about the Netzer not coming as a King to rid us of our Gentile oppressors. I was focused on Jacob's actions not the chaos around Isaiah. He picked up the scissors and put them in the sewing kit that was attached to his waist. And I need to add that as for motive, Jacob was aware of the threat of excommunication and I heard him say that he would not allow others to tell him where he could live."

Just then Joseph returned with the sewing kit and handed it to Jeremiah. Jeremiah began to loosen the drawstring but then stopped and asked Joseph. "Was it where you had left it? And have you opened it?"

"It was right where I placed it and I have not opened it."

Jeremiah opened the kit and reached in. He slowly pulled out the scissors. They were covered in dried blood.

James watched Jacob fall to his knees, shaking his head. The assembly surged forward and the guards had to protect Jacob from those who wanted to tear him to pieces. James, Judas, and Simon also rushed forward as well as others who were there to support Jacob. The supporters of Jacob surrounded him to protect him as those who wished him ill tried to beat him.

Jeremiah and Matthan were able to call the room to order by yelling out names and threats to those involved in the fighting. After 10 to 15 minutes of disorder Matthan was able to get everyone to stop pushing and move to separate parts of the room. He asked those who were angry with Jacob to keep to the back of the room and those who wished to protect him to come forward to the front near Jacob. This shuffle put James, Judas, and Simon directly behind Jacob with about 20 other men. James recognized them as Jacob's friends and those most likely to still believe that Jesus was the true Netzer.

Jeremiah spoke in a loud voice. "Men of Judah, We are not like the Gentiles who foolishly rush to violence when upset. I, like you, am disturbed by the evidence that we have uncovered but we have the law of the Almighty to guide us to truth! And we will follow the law!" And then more softly he spoke to Jacob who was standing on the floor in front of him. "Jacob the witnesses and evidence to convict you of the murder of Isaiah is before you. It is now your turn to offer your defense for attacking our Rabbi."

Jacob slowly ascended the bema and faced the Lesser Sanhedrin. "Men of honor," he began with a choked voice. "Our forefathers lived in this land for many years as aliens and were viewed as the outsiders even though the Almighty had promised this land to our father Abraham. It was only after our time of slavery in Egypt, from which we were rescued by the Holy One's strong arm that we were brought to this land again. He drove the inhabitants out and gave us safety in this land which flows with water every rainy season, is excellent for raising sheep, and produces crops of dates and wine and grain. It is a land flowing, with milk and honey."

"But it was through a great struggle that we inherited this land. And in that struggle we learned the role of the Passover Lamb. The Lamb was slain so that we could live. And we have been commanded to remember that sacrifice by regularly sacrificing other animals to atone for our sin so we may continue to live in this land. The Almighty took an alien family, built it into a nation, and gave it a home. But we always had the reminder that other lives, other blood, had to be spilled to keep us in this land and in right relationship with Him."

"I stand before you now accused of spilling the blood of Isaiah. But the real issue is that we have misunderstood the role of the Netzer. He is the promised prophet who will lead us out of bondage to sin just as Moses led us out of bondage in Egypt. He is the son of David who will rule in our lives as we submit to his authority. He is the son of the Almighty who will welcome all aliens into His promised land. He is the Passover Lamb who will shed his blood to save us from our sin. The Netzer is, as the Prophet Isaiah stated, the one who pours out his life unto death, and is numbered with the transgressors, he bears the sin of many, and makes intercession for the transgressors. He is Jesus of Netzereth."

Immediately the room exploded with shouts and a surge towards the bema. The friends of Jacob created a wall which kept the crowd from rushing the platform. But through this struggle James noticed that Jacob stood there with a calm look on his face which was tilted upward as if listening to a voice above.

Jeremiah and Matthan again quieted the assembly. And then Matthan asked, "We are well aware of your heretical beliefs Jacob but you are standing accused of killing our beloved Rabbi. What do you say about that?"

"I did not kill Isaiah. I never had my scissors out of my pouch. I do not know how blood got on them."

Judas stepped forward, "I wish to speak in defense of Jacob."

Jeremiah motioned for Judas to ascend the dais and stand with Jacob. As Judas climbed the three steps he was followed by James and Simon.

Judas faced the Lesser Sanhedrin and said, "Yesterday I was in the scriptorium reading the Prophet Isaiah when I heard two men enter the synagogue and speak about planting evidence in Jacob's sewing pouch to implicate him in the death of Isaiah."

Suddenly every man on the Lesser Sanhedrin gave their complete attention to what Judas was saying.

Matthan stood up, "And James and Simon were you there as well? Did you overhear this conversation?"

"No we were not there but Judas came and told us about it yesterday afternoon." James stated.

"Well then, as there was only one witness, this is inadmissible testimony as there needs to be at least two witnesses. And there have been at least three witnesses to the stabbing that Jacob committed."

Ezra stood, "Are you able to identify the two men who were speaking of implicating Jacob?"

"Yes," Judas responded, "they were Jeremiah and Matthan."

"That is a lie." Jeremiah shouted.

"Again, that is the word of one person." Matthan cajoled, "I assure all of you, there was never a conversation of the sort Judas and Jacob are claiming. We are looking for the truth and they are obviously searching for any way to throw suspicion off of Jacob."

"I am not so sure." Ezra responded. "I think we should explore this further."

"I believe we have heard enough foolishness." Jeremiah stated. "We have the testimony of several witnesses to what happened two days ago right here when Jacob brutally murdered Isaiah. So as Head of the Sitting I call on the Lesser Sanhedrin to judge. Is Jacob guilty of the murder of Isaiah? All who believe he is guilty please stand."

Quickly a majority of the 23 men stood and then slowly as they saw how the vote was going the last few also stood except for Ezra who remained in his seat.

"It is decided." Jeremiah bellowed. "Guards, take the prisoner to the storage room and keep him there as the Lesser Sanhedrin decides on his punishment."

As the two guards began to lead Jacob away through the crowd, some of the men began to spit on and push Jacob. Jacob's friends went to his aide and scuffles and fist fights broke out making the route to the storage room impassable. Fighting continued in the synagogue as the two guards and some of the Lesser Sanhedrin pushed their way through the crowd.

After Jacob and his guards made it into the storage room and shut the door on the crowd, the fighting began to subside. Finally Matthan and Jeremiah were able to get some order restored.

"Men of Netzereth." Matthan yelled. "You are not behaving as Netzerim should. We are people of the Book. We are the ones in all of Israel who live by the laws of Moses. It is obvious from your behavior here today that you need a cooling down time. So for the safety of everyone concerned I am requiring everyone who identified as a supporter of Jacob stay here in the synagogue until the sun reaches its peak. This will give each group time to put away their wrath and again seek the good of our community. So supporters of Jacob stay here, all others are dismissed. You will be informed of the decision of the Lesser Sanhedrin by town crier."

At that the synagogue emptied except for the supporters of Jacob. A guard was placed outside the door on the porch of the synagogue ostensibly to protect those inside. But everyone knew the tide had turned and now they were in peril of at least social action against them for supporting Jacob. And they began to turn on James.

"What do we do now James?"

"My wife and children need me. I supported Jacob and Jesus for this?"

"You should have warned us that Matthan and Jeremiah had framed Jacob."

"What good is there in believing in the Netzer now?"

"MEN." The booming voice of Ezra echoed off the walls of the room. "We are all here because we have believed the words of the prophets and the testimony of the family of Joseph and Mary as well as the many signs and words of Jesus. Now is not the time to turn on each other and forget how The Almighty has taught and led us. Rather it is the time to regroup, come out of hiding, and stand for what we know to be the truth." And then in a softer voice, as he had everyone's attention, he added, "We have about two hours before we are allowed to leave the synagogue. I suggest we use this time wisely by asking Our Defender for help and wisdom in dealing with today's events."

James watched as he saw every man in the room kneel and place their heads on the ground in supplication for Jacob, themselves, and their families. He too joined them and prayed for salvation.

CHAPTER 13

(Sunday Afternoon)

The Lesser Sanhedrin, minus Ezra, would have met in the synagogue to determine the fate of Jacob but that space was unavailable because of the quarantine of the Jesus followers. They met in the courtyard of Jeremiah's home. His home was near the southern cliffs of Netzereth along the way that led down to the plain of Esdraelon.

Matthan spoke first. "We have been given a solemn task today. We must decide the fate of not only the convicted murderer but also the future of Netzereth. And I know some of you are concerned that Elder Ezra decided to stay with the others in the synagogue thus invalidating our decision here today. But let me remind you that it was decided beforehand that we would seek justice based on the Law of Moses, and the Torah does not comment on the rules of a Sanhedrin. Also I must make you aware of some other dreadful news. A Cohort of Roman soldiers was spotted on the Way of the Sea headed towards our village."

Nervous and shocked looks spread through the Lesser Sanhedrin.

"Perhaps," Matthan continued, "this is the very threat that we were afraid of when we heard of Jesus' entry into Jerusalem. So we must deal with this issue now without the help of Elder Ezra who has made clear to all of us what side he is on."

"Thank you Rabbi Matthan," Jeremiah said before turning to the group of men. "We do have an important job to do. The Torah calls for an 'eye for an eye' so I suggest that the murderer be taken to the cliffs, thrown down and stoned to death. I further suggest that this be done quickly before the Roman Cohort arrives so that we can demonstrate to them our distance from the claims of Jesus to be our king."

"But Jeremiah," countered Elder Job, "wouldn't that inflame the Cohort more, as all capital punishments are to be handled by the Romans?"

"That is true, but we also know that the gentiles will readily look the other way when a 'happy accident' happens in their favor. Plus, we can, as part of our efforts to save Netzereth and the Netzerim, round up all the followers of the heretic among us and hand them over to the cohort for their justice. I have asked that all the names of the families that remained in the synagogue be written down. We now know for certain who still believes in Jesus' claim as the Netzer. By handing them over to the Cohort we distance ourselves even more from the trouble coming our way."

The time of prayer and reflection did as Elder Ezra had wished. The compatriots of Jacob found peace in laying their fears before the Almighty. They began to speak with excitement concerning Jesus the Netzer. They shared stories with each other about memories and encounters they had experienced with the Netzer. They began to dream again of the future when the Netzer would rule and restore Israel to the jewel it was in the Almighty's plan.

James appreciated the turn in mood but sat alone in thoughts of his own. Jacob's words about the suffering servant, the Passover Lamb, and forgiveness of sin, began to intertwine with James' memories of Jesus before he left home. Even an incident where a piece of limestone fell from its place and Jesus insisted on lifting the heavier portion so that James could have an easier lift, started to fit into the narrative of Jesus always serving others first. The remarkable way his brother made the stories of the past come alive in his retelling was remembered and enjoyed by James again. Jesus' love for him in finding the perfect wife for him reminded him of the generosity Jesus showed everyone who approached him with a need. James was glad Hadassah and Joshua and Sarah were safe but at the same time he knew Hadassah would love to hear these remembrances.

But, if Jacob was right about Jesus being a Passover Lamb, that would mean terrible things for him. Everyone around James was beginning to be encouraged by the faith of Jacob in the Netzer. But they were missing the point of Jacob's message. The Netzer was not a king in the earthly sense. But rather the Netzer was a king in the spiritual sense. He was to save people from the one enemy that plagued humanity since Adam and Eve. He was to be king in that all people would owe everything to him for saving them from sin. And he would do that through death.

James needed to get his mind and heart wrapped around this idea a bit more firmly. He searched the room for Ezra and Judas. No sign of them. Then he saw the barred door where Jacob was being held. A guard was leaning against it while speaking with Nathan, one of the twenty or so others waiting for permission to leave. He walked over to the guard and asked, "May I visit with Jacob?"

The guard paused in thought.

"Come on Benjamin, let him see his friend. What harm can it do?" Nathan asked.

Benjamin shrugged his shoulders and unbarred the door. James lifted the latch and opened the door with a quick "Thank you!" to both Benjamin and Nathan and walked in.

"James! So good to see you. Thank you for your support out there earlier. It got a bit tense for a while but I am sensing that the worst is over."

"Jacob, how can you say that? You have been convicted of murder. The Lesser Sanhedrin is right now deciding your fate and I don't think they are going to forgive you of murder."

"You're right. But I have such a joy right now because I was able to stand up for the Netzer in the face of fear. The Almighty gave me a peace, courage,… a conviction that

I was doing the right thing. I was playing my part in His grand design. I am elated that the Almighty has deemed me worthy to suffer for and serve His Netzer."

James shook his head in disbelief at what he was seeing and hearing. "I can't…. This is craziness. I came in here to cheer you up but instead you are strengthening me. The tone out in the assembly room is the same. There is a feeling of joy even though the worst possible situation surrounds us. What is happening?"

"I think it is the beginning of the Kingdom of the Name being brought into existence by the Netzer. He spoke of the Kingdom as if it was among us. He said that it was those who weep that would be comforted. He said the oppressed would see the salvation of the Lord. I really think we are seeing a glimpse of the Kingdom right here among us."

"Let's talk kingdom issues." James interrupted. "If Jesus is not an earthly king then how does he have a kingdom? If the Netzer is a lamb to be killed for the forgiveness of sin how is he supposed to reign as a king? How can my brother with all the promises and signs at his birth and obvious wisdom about the Almighty be the Netzer who is sacrificed, and reign over a kingdom?

"Look around you James. The answer is in these rooms. And in me in particular. When I refused your help last night to escape it was because I was serving my King. When I stood before the Lesser Sanhedrin and testified concerning the Netzer, I was under the rule of my True King. And even now, as I relive the joy of serving my King even though there is an impending doom, I give evidence that a truer Kingdom than Herod's or Caesar's is here in this room. How can the Netzer sacrifice his life and still be the King we have been seeking? I'm not entirely sure but I believe it can happen because this Kingdom is not of flesh and blood but of faith and truth. James, you must believe me when I say your brother is fulfilling all that the Almighty sent him to do as the Netzer and you can trust him. Just continue to do what he has asked of you, and you will be serving your Netzer King."

The smile on Jacob's face was huge. James could not escape the power of Jacob's faith in Jesus as the Netzer. In that moment James tore down the walls he had built inside and allowed the truth of Jacob's words and his brother's life, flood into his soul. James let out a big laugh and embraced Jacob.

After a long embrace, James held Jacob's shoulders at arms length and looked into Jacob's eyes. "The Netzer commanded me to stay strong and keep the family together. That is what I will do for my King." James kissed Jacob on both cheeks and determinedly walked out of the jail and into a new life.

Ezra and Judas had stolen themselves away to the Scriptorium. Judas wanted to get Ezra's opinion about the passage he had read yesterday when he overheard Jeremiah and Matthan plotting against Jacob. They read the passage again together and began to discuss what it meant and how it fit into Jacob's view of the Netzer. One particular section caused them much discussion.

> *For he was cut off from the land of the living: for the transgression of my people he was punished. He was assigned a grave with the wicked, and with the rich in his death, though he had done no violence, nor was any deceit in his mouth. Yet it was the Lord's will to crush him and cause him to suffer, and though the Lord makes his life an offering for sin, he will see his offspring and prolong his days, and the will of the Lord will prosper his hand. After he has suffered, he will see the light of life and be satisfied; by his knowledge my righteous servant will justify many, and he will bear their iniquities.*

"If... and that's a big if... we read this as referring to the Netzer rather than the traditional view of the suffering servant, there are some extreme concepts here. There is definitely a death that is ordained by the Almighty and that death acts as an offering for sin."

"I agree." Judas responded. "But there is also an indication of life after death. And not just any kind of life but a prosperous life, a satisfying life, a life with offspring. It does not sound like the afterlife of which the Sadducees deny and the Pharisees promise to their followers. It looks more like a coming back to life after being sacrificed. That is so unusual."

"And that is why the idea of the nation of Israel being the suffering servant is much more plausible. Our nation has died a number of times. The Assyrians destroyed Israel. Babylon destroyed Judah. And yet the Almighty has given our nation new life and prolonged our days."

"Yes but how has the death of our nation born our iniquities? And how can we say that our nation in the past had done no violence or deceit? It was because of their rebellion that the Almighty turned them over to their enemies." Judas pointed out the words on the scroll as he spoke.

Ezra sat in silence looking at the passage for a long time then finally said. "Either this passage is about the Suffering Servant Israel, who suffers to teach us the importance of staying pure before the Almighty and then we have the problem of the nation's obvious sin. Or the passage is about the Netzer who dies for the sin of Israel and yet lives."

After a pause Judas turned to Ezra and asked, "Do you believe that my brother Jesus is the Netzer of the Almighty?"

"Judas, if you had asked me that question two weeks ago, I would have said 'no'. And the reason would have been a poor one. I was part of the crowd that welcomed your parents and family back to Netzereth after their years in Egypt. I believed their accounts of angels, magi from the East and shepherds being told of his birth. I was committed to the idea that The Name would send a Netzer through our tribe of David to restore the kingdom. But the way he left us, moved to Capernaum, and became a Pharisee... set my nerves on edge. When he visited here and spoke in our synagogue without giving any evidence of his authority as he had done for other communities, he confirmed in my mind that he was a charlatan."

"So why are you locked in the synagogue with us heretics?"

"Because his triumphant entry into Jerusalem stirred in me the thoughts and feelings I had as a young man seeing your family return to Netzereth. I have spent this last week thinking through all the proof I had for his role as the Netzer before he began his public ministry. They all still ring true. In fact as I look at this passage in front of us I am reminded that I could find no violence or deceit in him. The one thing I had against him is my disappointment that he did not do what I thought he should do." Ezra paused and then turned to Judas with a smile, "But who am I to tell the Netzer, my King what to do. Yes Judas, I believe your brother, Jesus, is the Netzer of the Almighty."

Judas nodded and smiled back, "Me too."

Suddenly the curtain door was pulled back and one of the followers of the Netzer said, "We're free to go home now."

Simon sat alone in a corner of the assembly room. One phrase kept running through his mind, 'excommunication from the Netzerim'. Was that still the plan? Why else would they have all of us stay here in the synagogue? Maybe Matthan has in mind to carry out the excommunication of us all.

Maybe he has something even worse in mind. Something needs to be done to protect myself and my friends from these evil people.

When the doors were opened for the men to leave, Simon was the first one out and he ran all the way back to his work shed. There he gathered every knife and tool he could as a weapon and packed them into a leather bag. He was out of the family compound before James and Judas arrived. He headed to the hills above Netzereth to hide his arsenal and watch the village from above in secret.

The deliberations took much longer than anticipated. Jeremiah and Matthan had to keep steering the conversation back to the penalty for murder found in the Torah. The mention of the approaching Roman cohort had widely divergent impacts on the Lesser Sanhedrin. Half of the Sanhedrin was afraid of repercussions should the Romans find offense that they dealt with a murderer according to the Almighty's law. The other half believed the greater need was to appease the Romans concerning the 'triumphant entry' of Jesus of Netzereth into Jerusalem. It was two hours before they were finally able to reach a consensus about what to do with Jacob. In the end it was decided that he would be put to death the next morning.

But then the harder decision about what to do with all the Jesus followers in Netzereth had to be confirmed. Jeremiah,

Matthan, and a few others argued strongly for excommunication, seizing of their property, and redistributing it as the Elders saw fit. A small few argued that nothing needed to be done in as much as the execution of Jacob would be enough to demonstrate to the approaching Cohort that the town of Netzereth did not side with the heretic Jesus. In the end, after an unbearably lengthy debate, Jeremiah and Matthan agreed to just an arrest of the followers of Jesus and allow the Romans to decide what to do with them. Unfortunately, they arrived at this decision long after the guards had already released the men that had been held in the synagogue.

"News of our decision will spread quickly. So we must act quickly. Every man here who is willing to act on behalf of the Lesser Sanhedrin's decision should immediately arm themselves with a sword and a torch and in groups of three go to each of these homes." Jeremiah held up the list of names that had been written down earlier. "You are to bring the whole household to the synagogue tonight to be held there until the Roman Cohort arrives. And if you know of others not part of this Sanhedrin who would be willing to help you round up the followers of the heretic, get them to help you."

Matthan added, "We must act quickly so as not to allow any to escape justice. Now come to me and get your assignments."

CHAPTER 14

(Sunday Evening)

"**W**hy are we here Joseph? Couldn't we have gone to Cana instead? I have relatives there. We could have been with family. Instead we are surrounded by strangers." Hadassah whispered to Joseph, very conscience of the fact that they looked so out of place in the Gentile inn they had chosen to lodge in for the night.

Joseph sighed and said, "Hadassah, I've told you all I know. James wanted us to come to Sepphoris because of his connections here with some authorities. He did mason work here for one of the leading men of the city. He also wanted to talk to the Greek doctor that cares for the Roman magistrate here. He thinks the death of Isaiah was brought on by sickness. And to answer your latest concern, we are not in Cana because it's farther away and that would be one of the places Matthan would think to look for Jacob when my brothers rescue him. I realize they are very late in getting here but at least we are safe and we will move on after the rest of our family arrives."

Zerah approached Hadassah and Joseph from behind as they stared into the fire of the inn's courtyard. "The mattresses in our room are very comfortable. And Sarah and Joshua are already sound asleep." She sat down with Hadassah between her and Joseph. "Those two were worn out by our overnight trip. And then a whole day of playing in the courtyard here." Then lowering her voice she added, "Emma is just sitting in there depressed. I'm worried about her."

"She is separated from the two people she loves most in this world. She will cheer up when Jacob gets here." Then turning to Joseph, Hadassah added, "But they should have been here this morning. You don't think something has gone wrong do you?"

"It was a wild plan to begin with, but I know Simon, Judas, and James can pull it off. I'm going to sit up all night and wait for them right here. Perhaps they are waiting to travel under the cover of darkness. You two should go comfort Emma and get some sleep. I'll come get you as soon as they arrive."

The two women got up and started walking to the room. Hadassah put her arm around Zerah and said, "Come on sister. You are about to experience the joy of listening to the family of James snore through the night."

"Thanks. I like the sound of that. 'Sister', I mean. Not the snoring."

"*I love that girl.*" Thought Joseph. "*Come on James. Where are you?*"

All Netzereth was in an uproar. Eighteen families had been rounded up and placed in the assembly room of the synagogue. Most of the families came begrudgingly but quietly. A few needed the persuasion of sword point. In fact Saul had a deep cut on his right arm where a sword had been used to hurry him along. His family and others were gathered around him to offer help and to complain about the ill-treatment.

However, there were some noticeable absences. Jacob's wife Emma was missing as well as their son Jesse. James' wife Hadassah and his two children and two of his brothers were missing as well. Joseph had not been seen all day but Simon was in the assembly room during the trial and protective custody. So they knew Simon was nearby. Jeremiah ordered a home-by-home search for the missing people.

Matthan entered the room and there was a sudden chill on all conversations as everyone watched him walk to where James was sitting. Heber and Nathaniel followed closely behind and watched the rest of the room for any kind of sudden movement.

"James, where is your family?

"I'm not sure I should answer that question. Am I on trial now as well?"

"No James. No one is on trial," Matthan responded mockingly. "The trial ended hours ago and your friend, whom you defended, was found guilty. That took care of the murder charge. Now Netzereth has to defend itself against the threat of Roman reprisal for your brother's actions these last three years. So your trial was decided by the Lesser Sanhedrin as well. And all of you were found guilty of endangering the lives of all the Netzerim."

Then ascending the bema Matthan spoke to all the families in the assembly room. "You all have shown yourselves to be supporters of the heretic Jesus. Despite the warnings your Elders and Rabbis have consistently given you. Therefore it has been decided by the Lesser Sanhedrin that you are all to be turned over to a Roman Cohort which is on it's way here as we speak. They will decide what will happen to those who support the heretic Jesus."

A shout came from the back of the room. "Rabbi Isaiah would never have allowed this to happen."

"You brought this on yourself." Matthan responded. And then he, Heber, and Nathaniel walked out as women and children began to whimper and some men had to be restrained by their neighbors from attacking the three.

James looked over the crowd and surveyed the emotional destruction. Families huddled together in despair for their lives. Some men seethed with anger while others were near tears as they imagined what the Romans would do to them. The women tried to comfort their children while at the same time feared their homes they had worked so hard for could be swept away from them in one day. James thought of his own family. He was glad they were not in Netzereth but would he ever see them again? The whole atmosphere of the room had completely changed from the joy of four hours prior.

"James, what can we do? Can Jesus help us? Is there any hope?" The question came from Saul who had pulled himself away from his wife and children to approach the only one who might have an answer. "My family, James, is in your hands. Tell us what we can do. Can you keep our Netzer family together?"

James was reminded of the task Jesus had given him on the roof before leaving for Capernaum. 'You must be strong for our family' Jesus had made him promise. And Jesus was the Netzer. And this room was now the family of the Netzer.

He turned to Saul and said, "Brother, we must pray for the guidance of the Almighty."

James bounded up the steps of the bema and called for everyone's attention. "My family, we are in the midst of a great trial, a trial that is testing our faith in the Netzer of the Holy One. Before leaving Netzereth, my brother... our Netzer, promised me that we would face these trials and it would be my role to stay strong for the family and keep our family together. You are my family. We must stay strong in our faith of the Almighty's Netzer and ask the Holy One for the wisdom we need to survive this trial. He will give generously to all who ask for wisdom. I call on Elder Ezra to come up here and lead us in such a time of prayer. And pray for me as I believe the Glorious Name has already placed in me a seed of an idea to help us. Pray that He will give me the wisdom to develop this plan into a workable solution."

Ezra stood next to James and placed his hand on his head. "To the One who gives life and wisdom, bless this servant you have sent to be our help, and bless your servant The Netzer."

From his hiding place Simon watched as the families of those supporting Jacob were gathered once again in the synagogue. He began to plot a secret route through the village to the synagogue. If he could reach the synagogue without being seen he could possibly save everyone by surprising the guards and delivering weapons to the men being held captive. Unfortunately, every route required navigating through the marketplace where he could easily be seen. And there seemed to be a torch bearing group on every street of the village looking for more Netzer supporters.

In frustration Simon whispered, "Jesus, why did you bring this on us?" His thoughts turned to the many times his oldest brother got the attention of the people of Netzereth, making Simon invisible. Simon could remember various times when his accomplishments were overshadowed or devalued because Jesus was there. When Jesus left Netzereth, Simon finally had an opportunity to shine. He was good at his work. Many people said so. Well, it was time for Simon to shine now in a big way. "I have to find a way down there."

But then, another thought hit him. What if the instigators of this terrible day were taught a lesson about bringing pain into other peoples' lives? His attention turned to the home of Matthan. There was an easier path to that structure, and it did not require going through the marketplace. Maybe a show of force there can turn the fortunes of friends and family around. Simon began to calculate what he could do to Matthan that would change his mind about the people in the synagogue.

Jeremiah met Matthan, Heber, and Nathaniel as they exited the synagogue. "Did he tell you where his family is?"

"No. And I really didn't expect him to." Matthan responded. "Do we know where Hadassah's family is from?"

"I believe they live in Nain. And she has distant cousins in Cana." Heber said.

Matthan continued, "If they have left for either of those two towns then they are not our problem anymore but I am worried that Joseph and Simon have not been found yet. If the two brothers are with them we really do need to bring them back to finally deal with this heretic's family."

"Are you thinking of sending someone to bring them back?" Jeremiah asked.

Matthan nodded. "Heber and Nathaniel are you two up for some night travel? Take some men with you. If you can bring back the women and children do so, but especially bring the brothers back here."

"I'll go to Nain." Heber said.

"That leaves Cana for me. But shouldn't we be here for the execution tomorrow morning?" Nathaniel asked.

"No it is more important that we find the brothers. I have a feeling they are key for stomping out this imposter's faction and ending this threat to our way of life. Jeremiah and I will take care of the situation here. You two deal with the brothers."

Heber and Nathaniel nodded and walked away to recruit their armed bands.

"Jeremiah, come to my home for a quick meal we should discuss the execution tomorrow morning." Matthan turned and walked toward his home and Jeremiah followed.

Simon had begun his descent into town without the use of a torch to light his way. It was difficult to see where he was going but it was also difficult to be seen. He reached Netzereth without incident and needed only to navigate through two pathways to reach the home of Matthan. Most homes had firelight emanating from their courtyards but it was simple enough to keep to the shadows as he carefully weaved his way through the streets. He arrived at Matthan's home and was going to enter when he realized Matthan was not alone. Simon quickly knelt in the shadows and listened as Jeremiah and Matthan spoke.

"I think it is only fitting that Jacob be executed at the same place that the heretic he supports escaped judgment."

"I agree!" Jeremiah responded. "And the stoning should go without a hitch. But I am concerned that the task of convincing the Roman cohort of the necessity may not go well."

"We need not frame Jacob's death as a judicial matter when speaking with the Romans. What we need to demonstrate to them is that the man who has claimed to be king from our small village has just a few followers, and the most vocal one is no longer alive. Therefore, Netzereth is of no threat to their peace. Then, if they wish to take custody of the few followers that are left, they are welcome to do so."

"But what if they don't want to take custody of the followers of Jesus?" Jeremiah asked.

"Then we will deal with them by our laws by excommunicating them, confiscating their property, and redistributing it to those who have remained faithful to the Almighty and the Essene community we have here in Netzereth."

"And I will finally own the land that should have been in my family for years."

"Yes, Jeremiah, we will make sure you get Ezra's land. But why do you believe it should have been in your family all along?"

"My great-grandfather sold it to new Netzerim who arrived from Bethlehem and needed land to cultivate. My great-grandfather was more of a merchant than a farmer so he saw no harm in selling off some of the land. He didn't know he was selling the best of his farmland and thus our family suffered because of his bad choice. Now we will get it back and things will be better."

"But yet you are single and have no sons to pass on that land wealth." Matthan snickered and shook his head in amusement.

Jeremiah countered, "Oh, but that will be changing as well. I have been in talks with David Ben Jehoida about his daughter Zerah. I have convinced him to cancel the marriage contract with Joseph. I plan on being Joseph's replacement."

Outside, Simon had heard enough. He pulled a knife out of his sash and burst in through the door. "You two and your schemes have done enough damage to my family. No more." He yelled.

Simon lunged at the two who were standing on the other side of the meal table. The table kept Simon from reaching his targets but in pushing the table two simultaneous things happened. The lamp on the table went out leaving the room in darkness and both Jeremiah and Matthan were pinned between the table and the wall. Simon kept slashing with his knife occasionally making contact with someone's arm or hand. He knew he needed to get closer so he climbed onto the table and lunged at the spot he thought Matthan's body would be but the blade hit the wall and the knife fell from his hands. Upon hearing the knife hit the stone floor a mad scramble for the weapon began as well as fist fighting. When he felt the blade of the knife hit his shoulder, Simon realized that he was outnumbered and weaponless and that his best bet was to retreat and backed up just in time to avoid the thrust of Matthan's right hand which had found the knife.

"Ah ha, I got you now Simon." Matthan shouted.

Simon stumbled back to, and out the door, turned and ran out of the room. He could hear Matthan following for a short distance but then Matthan suddenly stopped his pursuit. Simon could hear Matthan calling for neighbors to help and quickly slipped into the darkness outside of Netzereth. His shoulder was in pain and he could feel the blood running down his arm as he climbed the hills to his hiding spot.

Matthan pursued Simon as far as the courtyard but stopped when he realized he couldn't catch him and Jeremiah was not behind him. He instead called for help and a lamp. Upon re-entering his home, he and a neighbor found Jeremiah lying in a pool of blood with Simon's knife sticking out of his chest.

The prayer of the captives in the synagogue lasted hours as families joined together and found comfort, peace, and encouragement. But it was interrupted by a bloodied and angry Matthan.

"James and Judas, you are under arrest."

Six men grabbed the brothers and pulled them from the groups where they were kneeling in prayer. They were forced outside, beaten, and thrown against the wall of the synagogue.

"Where are your brothers?" Matthan yelled.

James stared back in confusion. Obviously something tragic had happened. Matthan was enraged and holding a cloth to a bloody hand. The men holding him and his brother were threatening them with more blows. The people inside the synagogue were yelling, demanding that James and Judas be released.

Matthan put his face in front of James' and spoke softly and sternly. "Simon came to my home and attacked me. He killed Jeremiah. Now, where is he hiding?"

"I don't know." James responded. This earned him another punch to the face. "I don't know." He screamed.

Suddenly the door of the synagogue flew open and the captives flooded out. They surrounded the two brothers, pushing the men holding James and Judas to the ground and holding them there. Matthan, realizing the tide had turned, ran off with his men. The guards who had been watching the captive prayer meeting were escorted out of the synagogue and James and Judas were brought in.

"He has pushed this too far. He is now accusing your brother of killing an Elder of Netzereth." Saul bellowed. "We know Jacob is innocent, Simon is innocent as well." Many heads nodded in agreement with Saul. But James and Judas looked at each other with doubt.

"Simon has always had a more impulsive response to hardship. Perhaps he did something he shouldn't have done. But killing Jeremiah?" Judas sighed, "I just can't believe it. There must be more to the story."

Jacob, who had been released from his closet by the others, approached James and Judas. "Simon is innocent. I'm sure of it. But you must go find him. Now is your chance. Escape before Matthan returns with more men. Go, save yourself."

"Come with us Jacob. Your family needs you." James pleaded.

"You know I can't, James. I must follow the path the Almighty has laid out for me. I will keep speaking to the people of Netzereth about His Netzer."

"I will be here to support and protect him." Ezra announced. "I am still an Elder in this village. My authority still carries a little weight. And he's right. You need to quickly go and find Simon."

Judas and James reluctantly left the synagogue and kept to the shadows making their way towards their home. They soon realized that was not a good route as many of Matthan's supporters were also looking for Simon and of course the home was crawling with them.

"James, do you remember when we wanted to get away from Jesus and our parents when they would get in those reminiscing moods?" Judas whispered. "They would go on and on about the escape to Egypt, the visit by magi, the dreams of angels. So we would run up into the hills with our sisters and make up stories about our births. Maybe that is where we might find Simon now."

"You may be right. You should go up there and check it out. But we also need to get more help. And it is time to ask for help beyond these walls."

Judas looked at James quizzically.

James continued, "You go up in the hills and find Simon. Find out what happened and keep the two of you safe. I'm going to Sepphoris to get help from the Roman magistrate and the Greek doctor. This trial is more than we can bear by ourselves."

"I agree brother. Be careful."

The two brothers separated and prayed silently that the Almighty would guide the other's path.

In Sepphoris, Joseph prayed for his brothers.

In the hills above Netzereth, Simon prayed for his brothers.

CHAPTER 15

(Monday Morning)

It was early, before sunrise, when Judas finally found Simon sleeping in the crevice of a large limestone boulder. While Judas prepared a proper bandage for his wound, Simon shared his account of the foolish attack on Matthan.

Judas listened quietly. Although he would have never taken such a course, he understood what drove Simon to such action. It was clear that the whole ordeal the people of Netzereth were experiencing was not as a result of Jesus' claim to the throne of Israel but rather the selfish pride of a few leaders.

When Simon finished his recounting with tears in his eyes from the sorrow he felt, Judas asked, "What do you think we should do now brother?"

"I've been thinking," Simon paused and choked back a sob, "I've been thinking that I would love to ask Jesus what we should do. He always knew how to make things right. I have failed him."

"How have you failed him?"

Simon looked square into the eyes of Judas. "Before Jesus left Netzereth he came to me in my workshop. He told me how much he loved me. He said that I had a courageous spirit that under the control of the Spirit of the Almighty, could be used to turn the hearts of many back to the Father. He said that he saw great things for me in the future but I needed to learn humility. And he said he would be watching to see how I would grow into the man he knew I could be." Simon paused. "It was just one month later that he moved to Capernaum. He understood me. He knew that I struggle with my anger. He always had just the right words to help me see a better way. I wish he were here right now."

Judas put his arm around his brother. "We all knew that you struggle with your anger." He gave Simon a hug and a smile. "But you are right, our brother always knew what to say and do, and I think he might be speaking to us even now."

Simon looked at Judas quizzically. "What do you mean?"

"Jesus also had a talk with me before he left. He said that the Almighty had blessed me with the ability to understand the deep secrets of His will. To be honest I was a bit confused by that statement. I laughed at him when he said it. But then he went on to say that knowledge without wisdom and courage could become toxic. I asked him what he meant and he explained it like this. Understanding the truth without wisdom will lead to abuse of power. Understanding of truth without courage will lead to stagnation. I believe I know what he meant. I have always enjoyed reading the prophets and digging into the depths of Scripture and who the Almighty is. But if I don't gain wisdom on how to use the truth I can abuse it. I think that is what we see Matthan doing." Simon nodded in agreement.

Judas continued, "But knowledge of the truth without courage to speak the truth will lead to a life that is dead. I need to speak the truth. And the truth is that Jesus is the Messiah, the Netzer." Judas stood and held out a hand to Simon. "So brother, I think Jesus is talking to us now. He wants you to employ some humility in your courage by turning yourself in and telling your side of the story. And he wants me by your side, borrowing from your courage to tell the truth about who Jesus is and who Matthan is."

Simon grabbed Judas' hand and was pulled up. They embraced and began their descent into Netzereth.

James found Joseph asleep at a burned-out fire in the courtyard of the inn. He shook Joseph gently. "Wake up Joseph, wake up." he whispered.

Joseph slowly opened his eyes and said "Well, finally. What time is it?"

"It's just after dawn. I traveled all night to get here. Where are the women and children?"

"They are safely tucked away in the room we rented." Joseph sat up and looked around. "Where are the men?"

"Things did not go as planned."

"I figured, since you are a whole day late. What happened?"

James sat next to Joseph on the bench on which he had fallen asleep. "Everything was perfect until Jacob refused to be rescued."

"He did what?"

"He wouldn't come with us. We would have made a clean escape from Netzereth but Jacob said that Jesus wanted him to stay and witness for him at the trial."

"He saw Jesus?" Joseph interrupted.

"No. It was more that Jacob knew what Jesus would want him to do based on who he believes Jesus to be and the teachings he has given. And although," James began to smile, "circumstances don't look good right now I believe Jacob was right."

"I don't understand brother. Is Jacob safe or not and where are Judas and Simon?"

"In quick summary here is what has happened because we must hurry, Jacob was tried for the death of Isaiah and found guilty." James waved aside with his hand the obvious questions that came to Joseph's mind and continued. "The believers in Jesus' claim as Netzer Messiah were rounded up in the synagogue to await the arrival of a Roman cohort. Simon was not part of the group in the synagogue as he was in hiding. And then late last night Matthan accused Simon of attacking him and Elder Jeremiah in his home and killing Jeremiah. Judas is looking for Simon in the hills above Netzereth and I came here to check on you and to get help." James put his hands on Joseph's shoulders as he was beginning to jump with questions and fears. "I have a plan brother. We need help and I believe our acquaintances here in Sepphoris may be able to save our whole family. But we must move quickly. I'll explain the plan to you as we go." James stood and began to walk to the rooms of the inn.

"Go where?" Joseph said following.

"First to the magistrate's doctor. Which room is our family in?"

Joseph pointed to the door. James walked to it and quietly knocked. "Hadassah?" he whispered.

"James!" came her excited reply and the door opened as she exited and closed it behind her. They embraced and she whispered, "I was so worried for you husband."

James released his embrace and held her by her shoulders putting his forehead on hers. "Listen carefully. We are not completely safe yet. Jacob has been found guilty of murdering Isaiah, and Simon is also in big trouble. I need to get back to Netzereth with help. I need to take Joseph with me right now but he will stay to protect you all as I return to Netzereth to save Jacob and Simon. But this is the important thing I wanted to tell you." He paused and his eyes brightened as a big smile came over his face. "My brother Jesus is the Netzer Messiah, who will save us all from our sin."

Hadassah's eyes grew big as she saw the change in her husband and she jumped up and hugged her man around his neck. James lifted her off her feet and spun her in a circle before setting her down.

"But I must hurry dear. We will talk about it all when we are safe." Then turning to Joseph he said, "Come brother I need your help." And he started walking out of the inn's courtyard.

Hadassah looked at Joseph with a big smile and he returned a confused look and a shrug and quickly followed after James.

Jeremiah's body was prepared for burial and placed in the family tomb. His sisters and their families wailed as the rest of the community tried to comfort them. Matthan read Scripture and prayed for those gathered but his attention was elsewhere.

Aside from the guilt of knowing that his hand had actually killed Jeremiah he was tormented with the crushing weight of trying to orchestrate the execution of Jacob on his own and convince the approaching Roman cohort of the innocence of Netzereth in Jesus' claim to the throne. His hatred of the whole family of Jesus was beginning to boil over and so he had to be mindful of how he proceeded so that he would come out of this whole mess as the hero of the Netzerim.

As soon as he could, he gathered the remaining elders of Netzereth and convinced them of the necessity of following through on the planned execution that morning. They also listened to the reports of those who were actively searching for Simon and the rest of the escaped brothers. There were two armed bands of men searching Netzereth and the surrounding countryside for any of the brothers and a watch was also put on their home. So far there had been no sign of any of them. Matthan secretly hoped that they had all fled far away and out of his life forever.

With the elders' approval to continue with the stoning of the murderer of Isaiah, Matthan ordered the transport of Jacob to the cliffs above Netzereth.

Elder Akim, newly appointed head Elder, read the verdict of the Lesser Sanhedrin as Jacob stood facing the stone carrying crowd with his back to the thirty foot cliff. After reading the verdict Akim allowed Jacob to have one final word before his execution.

"Men of Israel", Jacob began, "I am innocent of the charges against me. I had no reason to kill Isaiah. I loved the man. As I also love all of you and want you to return to a knowledge of the truth that Jesus of Netzereth is the Netzer Messiah. His entry into Jerusalem to fulfill the prophecy of Zechariah was not a political declaration but rather a relational and spiritual declaration. Jesus is not our political king. He is the king of our hearts and lives. He has come to save us from ourselves, our sin, not the Romans." Jacob paused and searched the eyes of those in front of him. "I can see that I have not convinced any of you, and that makes me sad. But if I need to die for the king of my life, I am ready to do so. But know this; the child who grew up here in Netzereth and was supported by many of you is now fulfilling the Scriptures you have pledged to uphold. Killing me will not stop the work he was sent here to do as the Netzer Messiah."

"I have heard enough." Matthan yelled as he raised a stone above his head.

Others also raised their rocks but a shout from their right stopped the execution.

"Wait. Let me speak." It was Judas. He was standing on a large rock formation above the crowd with Simon at his side.

"It's Simon. Arrest him." Matthan shouted.

"Hold." Judas retaliated as he held up his hand as a signal to the crowd to stop. "We will be heard. Simon has confessed to me that he did attack Matthan and Jeremiah last night. But Jeremiah died at the hand of Matthan not my brother."

Heads turned to look at Matthan.

"Lies. He attacked us. He's the murderer. The whole family of Jesus are murderers. They will destroy Netzereth." Matthan ranted on uncontrollably and more and more men in the crowd looked at Matthan with concern. When Matthan saw the looks he stopped suddenly and then repeated, "Arrest him."

"Men of Netzereth, Simon was outside Matthan's home last night when he overheard Matthan and Jeremiah speaking of their plan to confiscate the property of all the followers of Jesus for their own gain. He also learned of the desire of Jeremiah to steal our brothers betrothed from him. We have just visited David, the father of Zerah, and confirmed that Jeremiah approached him, asking him to break the marriage covenant he had with Joseph our brother. David admitted that he was also promised more land in Netzereth once the followers of Jesus were excommunicated."

"Is this all true Matthan?" Elder Akim asked.

"Truth? Here's the truth. You were all there. You saw the trial which convicted Jacob of Isaiah's murder. You know he is guilty. You also know that the false messiah Jesus has deluded too many of the people of Netzereth for far too long. Jacob has been sentenced to death. Jesus is bringing death to our village and the words of his family are causing all of you to doubt again the righteous, just, punishment for heretics who lead our nation away from the Almighty. Jesus slipped through your fingers once on this very spot by causing you to doubt your righteous duty to the true Netzer Messiah. Don't let it happen again." Matthan's face was red with rage as he finished screaming.

Suddenly he turned and faced Jacob who had not moved during the whole debate and said, "In the name of justice and righteousness, I condemn you for the murder of our Rabbi by casting the first stone." The stone hit Jacob squarely on the forehead and was followed by several other stones which caused Jacob to stumble backward and fall off the cliff. His body hit the base of the cliff with a loud crack and was soon covered with a barrage of large stones as most of the men in the crowd joined in the execution.

"What do you hope to accomplish by talking to the doctor? Is Simon ill?" Joseph was walking quickly to keep up with James and had to speak a little loudly for the early morning.

"No Joseph. Simon is not sick, at least not that I know. I want to ask the doctor about Isaiah's death. I believe he may be able to give us some insight into what actually happened. After speaking with the doctor, we will go to the magistrate and ask for his assistance in fixing the struggle in Netzereth."

Joseph grabbed James by the elbow and pulled him to a stop. "Are you crazy? The Roman threat is what started this whole mess we are in."

"Joseph, Jesus is not a threat to the Romans. Think about it. He rode into Jerusalem on the colt of a donkey not a mighty fighting steed. The Romans won't understand the symbolism that we apply to the 'triumphant entry'." James shook his head and snickered. "Isaiah sure knew how to create a word picture. If the Roman authorities ask our Jewish brethren what the event meant they will either hide the significance for fear of reprisal or explain it away as the actions of a madman. And we know Jesus did not do it to start a rebellion because he has not prepared or given any speeches about rebellion. In fact Jacob confirmed with us that the time that he fed all those people by the Sea of Galilee and they wanted to make him king, he left them, and refused the honor. Instead, I have become convinced by Jacob that Jesus is the Netzer Messiah in a different way. He is the Lamb who takes away the sin of the world. I'm not exactly sure what that means but I aim to seek him out and ask my brother face to face once we are through this trial."

"Then why is there a Roman cohort on the way to Netzereth right now?"

"I don't know." James replied flippantly. "And I don't care. Roman squads are constantly patrolling the villages and country roads of our land. They might just be passing through. But I am sure that Matthan will use their presence as an opportunity to cause our family and all who believe in our brother more trouble. So we need some Roman authority on our side."

"But James, the Romans? How about the Zealots instead?"

"Do you know any Zealots nearby Joseph?" James gave him a sideways glance indicating he knew there would be a negative response. "We have here in Sepphoris, Roman citizens who know us, trust us, and might be willing to come to our aid. And they are important Romans who can with a wave of their hand end our struggle in Netzereth."

James saw the fear in Joseph's face. "Do you remember the time we were hired to build the new pot chamber in the magistrate's home?" Joseph nodded and let out a big sigh. "Of course you do. The magistrate wanted the privy to be a smaller size than the original but we both knew that it needed to be at least the same size as the old one because of the girth of his wife." Both of men laughed at the remembrance. "I sent you to tell him the bad news but you were afraid to deal with it, so I had to do it. I found the magistrate to be understanding if just a bit upset. I also found out he wanted a smaller privy so he would have room for other improvements. We sat down together and I showed him how we could change the orientation of the privy, keep it the same size, and provide room for the other things he was looking for. Roman authorities don't have to be our enemies Joseph. The Name places others in authority over us and we are asked to obey out of respect but that does not mean we are to fear them." James paused to let the words sink in a bit and then added. "By the way I am very proud of you for standing up to David and holding him to the marriage contract we made with him. By taking the lead in bringing our family to safety here in Sepphoris, along with Zerah, you have shown great growth."

James knew that his words hit home with his brother. And he slapped him on the shoulder. "Come, we're here at the doctor's home."

They approached the courtyard gate and knocked. A male servant opened the gate and asked, "May I be of service?"

"We would like to speak with the doctor. Is he available?"

"I'm sorry no. He is still in his bed chamber and has asked not to be disturbed." The servant began to shut the gate but James put his foot against it keeping it open. "Please we need to speak with him. It will only take a moment of his time. My name is James of Netzereth and this is my brother Joseph. We need the doctor's expertise on a matter of some importance."

"You are from Netzereth?"

"Yes but that doesn't matter. We need to speak with the doctor and it will only take a bit of his time."

"Do you know Jesus of Netzereth?"

James took a step back and responded slowly. "Yes. He is my older brother."

Suddenly the gate swung open wide and the servant smiled widely and exclaimed, "Please come in. Have a seat by the fire. We have bread and water and grapes and figs and quail available. Are you hungry? May I serve you something while you wait for the doctor?"

James and Joseph entered and sat at the fire in shock over the reception. Joseph asked, "Do you know our brother Jesus?"

"Oh no. I've never met him. But I know of him. Let me inform my master that you are here to speak with him and then I would love to tell you my story, if that's okay?" The servant walked away without waiting for an answer but instead called two other servants. "Elizabeth, Rachael, bring these men some food and drinks please." And then he disappeared into the house.

Judas and Simon ran into Netzereth as quickly as they could to escape the mob but found no place to hide. They soon found that they were trapped, and the only safety they could hope to have would be with the others in the synagogue. They approached the front doors and the guards who were unaware of the events on the cliff were surprised to see the two of them and gladly allowed them to enter the synagogue.

The others in the synagogue were also surprised to see them and began throwing questions at them. Judas and Simon were able to confirm that Jacob had indeed been executed and Elder Ezra led everyone in prayers for his family. They were also able to explain the events of the night before and the truths they had learned about the motives of Matthan and Jeremiah and possibly other leaders. The atmosphere in the room was somber and sorrowful. Simon especially noticed the absence of anger and instead saw small family groups huddled in prayer for their safety but also the safety of their friends on the outside who had been supporting the leadership of Matthan and Jeremiah.

"I think I am beginning to see the change that happens when anger doesn't rule your life." He said to Judas quietly. "I'm going to go join some friends in prayer."

Judas watched his brother sit with a family and admired the new Simon he was seeing.

"I might owe Simon a debt of gratitude." Elder Ezra said as he came up behind Judas. "Now that I know what was really going on it makes more sense to me. Jeremiah has referred a number of times to the sale of his family's land to my family and I always knew there was a bit of regret there. But I had no idea how much he was tormented by it."

Judas turned to face him and nodded agreement.

"Do you have any idea what James' plan is and how we are going to get through this trial?" Ezra asked.

"I'm sorry, I don't know. But I do know he will be back and he will bring an answer. James has always been able to work out a solution to keep his family strong. And we all," Judas gestured to the whole room, "are his family."

James and Joseph were enjoying fresh grapes, figs, and dates with cool water when the servant approached them at the fire.

"My name is Petros. I am the head servant for my master Heretas who is the personal physician of Magistrate Gaius." Petros sat down opposite James and Joseph with a big smile and continued, "My master will see you but only briefly as he has business to attend to elsewhere. But as he is still preparing for the day we have some time to talk. I have a brother who lives in Capernaum. He has written often to me about your brother Jesus of Netzereth."

"Yes, our brother moved from Netzereth to Capernaum and I hear he has a big following there." James explained.

"Well my brother, Antony, is not a follower but is a big admirer of your brother. And so am I as a result." James and Joseph gave a confused look to Petros and he continued. "I love my brother dearly. He raised me as a child as our parents died when we were young. We had to become servants to the wealthy in order to survive. Antony watched over me and taught me how to serve with excellence. We both excelled at our tasks and were hired to serve a Roman Centurion in Macedonia. We served him there together for three years and then he was transferred to Capernaum. Shortly after our arrival in Capernaum I was sent here to serve Heretas, who had just arrived from Athens to be the physician of the Magistrate. My brother and I have kept in contact these six years that we have been apart."

"How does a servant of a Roman Centurion meet our brother?" Joseph asked.

Petros smiled again and excitedly said, "It was a miracle. My brother was ill. So sick that everyone in the household thought he would die. Even my master went to minister to him and there was no change. But Cretius, that's the Centurion my brother serves, would not give up. He had heard about your brother and had even heard him teach on several occasions. He sent word through some Jewish leaders to Jesus asking him to heal my brother and Jesus agreed to go to a Roman home to heal him. Cretius was shocked that a holy rabbi would be willing to enter a Gentile home and sent word that he understood that Jesus had authority to heal and that all he had to do was say it was so and it would be done. You know, in the same way a master says to a servant 'do this' and it is done. Cretius knew that Jesus could just say the words and it would be done. Jesus healed my brother. He did it without seeing him. Without touching him. Your brother saved my brother's life." The joy was overwhelming on the face of Petros as he shared his story.

James and Joseph sat in shock looking at a man who was bubbling with excitement and joy. Then suddenly his demeanor changed and he stood and announced, "Master Heretas, these are the men who are here to speak to you." Then he bowed and walked away.

James and Joseph stood and turned to see the physician Heretas standing behind them with a foot soldier just behind him.

"I don't have much time and I would have sent you away but my servant insisted I speak with you. So what do you want and be quick about it."

In a quick conversation with Heretas, James and Joseph learned that there was no definitive proof that Isaiah had died of any kind of sickness but the doctor was intrigued with the fact that Isaiah seemed to be in some pain and that he was a man of big size.

"I have seen other cases where people who are fatter than normal can die suddenly after experiencing pain in their arms. I don't know the cause or how to prevent it but I have seen it happen."

"Thank you doctor, that was helpful." James responded.

After Heretas had left, James and Joseph headed to the courtyard gate and were stopped by Petros.

"May I ask what that was about? I heard bits of the conversation but I'm curious and I would love to be of help to the brothers of Jesus if I can."

"I don't think there is anything you can do. The man who died was our village rabbi and a friend was accused of causing his death. I was hoping the doctor could give us a clear statement saying that he died of a sickness. But unfortunately he couldn't. So now we are going to see Magistrate Gaius to see if he can intervene in the events happening in Netzereth."

"Oh James," Petros responded, "I'm sorry the Magistrate is not here. He is in Caesarea on business for Rome."

"Now what are we going to do brother?" Joseph asked.

After a pause in which James seemed to be looking for an answer to his dilemma right there in the courtyard, Petros interjected excitedly, "I might have an answer for you."

CHAPTER 16

(Monday Afternoon)

Judas watched from a distance as the two Elders had a discussion which was at times heated, about the news of Jeremiah's desire to obtain Ezra's land. Akim had arrived twenty minutes earlier and asked to speak with Ezra privately. In the end, they both stood and embraced and Judas watched Akim leave the synagogue. But before the guard closed the front door behind Akim, the lead Elder of Netzereth turned and surveyed the room of some forty to fifty men, women, and children and his face displayed concern.

A small crowd of men had gathered around Ezra to hear if there was any hope for them and their families. Judas walked over to join them.

"Elder Akim is a good man. He doubts that Jesus is the Netzer but he does not let that color his thinking or concern for all the Netzerim. He will personally check into the information Simon has brought us about Matthan and Jeremiah." Ezra shrugged and continued, "We will see if this changes our situation. I don't know."

Judas turned away as others continued to ask Ezra questions. He began to rethink how things could have gone differently if he and his brothers had, as their mother had done, followed Jesus and agreed with his decision to move to Capernaum. What if he had seen the suffering servant passages and the messianic passages differently, as he does now? Could they have avoided all this turmoil? Could they have saved Netzereth from this civil war? Why didn't Jesus make it clearer to them before beginning his teaching ministry? But, how did their mother see the truth and follow when the rest of the family did not?

He thought back to his memories of everyday life with the whole family together. He conjured up pictures in his mind of playing in the courtyard with Jesus, his other brothers and sisters and mother and father watching them from the door of their room. "They loved us with an undying love." he whispered to himself.

Relationships, that's what mattered! The reason mother followed Jesus is because of her unfailing relationship with him. She was as confused as we were with his initial actions but that didn't interfere with her believing him to be the Netzer. We can have all the knowledge of the world but it is relationships that win the day. It is my relationship with the Almighty, my faith, that determines my obedience. Knowledge supports my faith. But my faith is built on relationship.

Judas fell to his knees and prayed. "Almighty God, throughout our history you called us into relationship with you. You are my Father. You are my Mother. You are my Protector. You are my Love. You are seeking relationship with me. I accept. You sent Your Netzer to be my Brother, my Friend, my Redeemer. I accept. Thank you for wanting me. I want You. I will follow You and Your Netzer. My Brother." Judas noticed that he had finished his prayer with a big smile on his face. "And that is what a relationship can do." He exclaimed out loud.

"He did what?" Hadassah screamed at Joseph as she ran to the courtyard gate.

"He's gone Hadassah. They had to hurry in order to save Jacob and Simon. He will be back for us. This will work. Matthan and the Elders can't refuse the word of a centurion soldier."

"What is going on?" Emma emerged from their room with Zerah and the children following. "Where is James?"

"He is on his way back to Netzereth…"

"With a Roman Centurion." interrupted Hadassah. "Joseph, how could you let this happen?" Hadassah started to cry. Emma and Zerah came to her side and hugged her.

Joseph looked at the three women and continued, "I know this is shocking news but please just listen to me… please?" Joseph motioned for the women to sit and when everyone was settled he continued. "We visited the home of the Magistrate's physician. While there we met his head servant who used to serve a Centurion of Capernaum. That Centurion happened to be here in Sepphoris to receive orders for the sea area over which he has authority. That Centurion is also familiar with the ministry of Jesus and has had positive relations with Jesus. Jesus healed his head servant in an astounding way. Cretius, the centurion, was leaving today to go back to Capernaum and when he heard of our situation he was more than happy to adjust his route back to Capernaum to include a stop in Netzereth."

Joseph looked at the three women and they continued to stare back at him with raised eyebrows. Joseph sighed, "He's a great guy. He loves our people, our land. He built the new synagogue in Capernaum. You know me Hadassah. I am the one who distrusts authorities, especially Roman authorities. But I'm telling you this guy Cretius, is on our side."

"I believe you Joseph." Emma responded. "In fact, you have given me hope that I will be reunited with my husband soon. Thank you." Emma stood and said, "It's in the Almighty's hands. We must attend to what is before us today." She looked down at Joshua and held out her hand. "And I believe that is a trip to the marketplace to buy food for today. Come along Joshua, what are we going to get at the market today?"

"I want grapes." He responded with enthusiasm.

Hadassah stood, wiped her eyes and looked at Joseph, shaking her head. "I hope you're right. And there better be grapes at the market." She beamed a big smile at Joseph and he let out a huge laugh as she turned to join the others leaving the courtyard.

Matthan stood at the doorway of his home sipping a glass of wine. One of the major events of the day had been carried out, although a bit sloppily, he reasoned. The other main event was soon approaching. The Roman cohort would be in Netzereth before sunset today and he had to have all his wits about him to see Netzereth rid of the corrupting vermin currently contained in the synagogue. But the loss of Jeremiah was a big blow. And with Heber and Nathaniel out searching for the missing family of Jesus, Matthan found himself a bit short-handed. He did still have the ears of a majority of the people. That was evident from the barrage of stones that followed his in the execution. But in dealing with Romans, you could not count on the strength of your numbers. Romans worked under a different mindset. They struck first and asked questions later. This put fear into the people and fear brought hesitation and he who hesitates fails. Matthan could not fail. The future of the Netzerim depended on him getting this done right.

Matthan drank the last bit of wine in the cup and set it down. In order to have the upper hand with the Romans he had to be the first to speak with them. He had to have sentries on the roads to Netzereth who could warn him of the cohort's approach. He headed out of his home to recruit the four men he needed to watch the roads.

The trip from Sepphoris to Netzereth was going much faster than it had ever gone before for James. Of course, this was the first time he had done the five-mile distance on horseback. In company with him were Cretius and three other mounted soldiers.

Cretius was speaking and had been for much of the trip so far. Everything he said was said with a tone of excitement and wonder. "So that is when I decided to check into the religion of the Jews. I mean think of it. Everywhere else in the Empire the conquered peoples have been required to make sacrifices to the emperor. But here, Julius Caesar, Mark Antony, Claudius, and even Augustus have made statements allowing for the Jews to worship according to their own customs. What is so special about this religion? I had to find out. And then, your brother shows up. At first we were wary. He was gathering larger and larger crowds. And that is never a good thing from a policing point of view. So, I watched him carefully. The reports I kept getting were that he spoke with authority about the Scriptures so I asked for the Scriptures that he was referring to in his teaching. I was amazed at what I was learning. And when Antony became sick and death seemed not far away, I turned to the man who had authority, your brother. Ah… there it is." Cretius pointed down the hill to the small village of Netzereth.

"Do you see that Cretius?" asked the lead rider.

On the road before them in the distance two men who were sitting on a rock near the road had suddenly jumped up and ran into the village.

"I see. It's somewhat of a typical response from country people seeing the approach of a Roman soldier. But it could also mean we were expected."

James noticed the change in Cretius' voice and posture and was glad that this time the Romans were the good guys.

A few minutes later they were greeted at the edge of Netzereth by Matthan and most of the Elders of the village. When Matthan saw James riding with the Roman soldiers his brow furrowed and he stumbled out his greeting.

"We are the… leaders of Netzereth… Why have you come to our village?"

Cretius dismounted and approached Matthan. "We are here to investigate the incarceration of a man named Jacob and those who claim to be followers of Jesus of Netzereth."

Misunderstanding the intentions of Cretius, Matthan replied, "Yes we have the traitors locked up in our synagogue for you to take into custody."

"And why would I want to take them into custody? What have they done?"

Matthan looked at James and back at Cretius. "I first wish to thank you for capturing one of the men we have been looking for. He and the others believe that the traitor Jesus is the King of the Jewish people. That his demonstration a week ago was a signal to the Jewish people to take up arms against the armies of Caesar. We as the leaders of Netzereth repudiate the kingly claims of Jesus. And as a sign of our loyalty to Rome we have rounded up those among us who still follow this traitor Jesus."

James noticed with a bit of amusement the uncomfortable looks of some of the elders when Matthan mentioned their loyalty to Rome.

Cretius continued "So their crime is belief that Jesus is their king. They have not actually taken up arms against Caesar as of yet?"

"No, we have kept them in the synagogue under guard so that they would not have the chance."

"Well done. And what is your name sir that I may report to Caesar your role in stopping this uprising."

James had to hide his own smile as Cretius had correctly seen Matthan's vanity.

Matthan answered, "My name is Matthan. I am the newly appointed lead Rabbi of Netzereth. And these men with me are the Elders of the village."

"Very good." Then turning to his soldiers and James still mounted on their horses he said, "Janus, please record Matthan's name in our records and make sure you keep an eye on that traitor." And then he winked at James.

Turning back to Matthan he said, "Please show us the way to the synagogue."

Hadassah and Emma strolled through the marketplace keeping a close eye on Joshua who was jumping from booth to booth petting every goat, lamb, and bird he could get his hands on. Sarah was ahead of them being held by Zerah as she and Joseph shopped and laughed together.

"They do make a good-looking couple." Emma said looking at the threesome as they fed Sarah some obviously sour grapes and laughed at her reaction.

"Yes they do!" Hadassah responded. "And it is good to see them enjoying each other given the turmoil at home." Then placing her hand on Emma's shoulder she added, "And it's good to see you enjoying life a bit more today also."

"James' arrival and news has given me hope. I am still very concerned for Jacob and Jesse but at least I know Jesse is not in Netzereth. And although I was upset that Jacob did not come to me in Sepphoris I am heartened by his desire to speak for Jesus as the Netzer, as the lamb who takes away the sin of the world."

"It is wonderful to see you so optimistic and to see the joy when you talk about Jesus. But I must say your faith that all will be well is stronger than mine, Emma."

"My confidence is in the One and in His Netzer, and in my place with Him, with Jacob's place with Him. Things may not go as I hoped but I know things will go as the Almighty plans. And I take joy in knowing that He cares for me and my family." They took a few steps in silence and then Emma said, "And I am so excited to hear that James has finally seen Jesus as the Netzer as well."

Hadassah smiled and nodded, "Me too. That was the best news. I can't wait to sit down and hear how that change happened. I am so excited. Do you think I could convince him to take the family to Jerusalem to tell Jesus ourselves? I would love to be in the same room with Jesus again and enjoy his company. It would be such a change from how we last left things with him."

"Only if my family can come with you." Emma replied excitedly. "Oh, maybe Jesse is with him right now."

The two friends looked at each other with smiles and silent excitement. But then Hadassah remembered something.

"Well, wasn't the plan for Jesse to get my father to send a messenger to Jesus. And for Jesse to stay with my family in Nain?" Hadassah asked.

"That was the plan." Emma replied with a smirk. "But I think I know Jesse pretty well. I wouldn't doubt that he somehow convinced your father to let him go as well."

"Well, I know my father pretty well. And I think Jesse is being kept safe and sound in Nain."

The two stopped and looked at each other, laughed out loud and embraced.

"Come on shmeeka." Hadassah called to Joshua. "Let's go catch up to your uncle and sister and have a snack back at the inn."

Joshua left the pen of lambs he had been standing near and ran to his mother's side.

Cretius had stationed two of his soldiers outside at the door of the synagogue while he took James and Janus into the assembly room. He demanded that Matthan and the Elders remain outside while he spoke with the captives.

Elder Joseph shook his head in sorrow as he watched the soldiers standing guard at the door. He turned to Matthan and lamented, "You realize we will now have to clean the synagogue from top to bottom now that this Gentile scum has made our worship area unclean."

"It could not have been helped." Replied Matthan. "We will take all the appropriate action we need to but we must get through this threat first." He paused in thought then stamped his foot and clenched his fists. "I did not expect the Centurion to exclude us from his interview of the heretics. I want to know what is being said in there."

Inside the synagogue Judas and Simon welcomed James with an embrace and the sad news of Jacob's execution. They were also surprised that he was accompanied by a Roman centurion.

"They are here to help us, brothers. I was hoping to get here before the execution so we could save Jacob but now we need to focus on the safety of the rest of our family. Cretius will want to know everything that has happened here. He is a fair man and he has had a wonderful interaction with our brother Jesus."

James bounded up the steps of the bema and called for everyone's attention. "Friends, family, the Almighty has been with me. Thank you for your prayers on my behalf. I am sorry I was not able to return in time to stop the death of our friend Jacob. But the One has provided us an answer to our need in the form of this wonderful centurion. There is no need to fear him. He also loves Jesus and would probably love to share with you the experience he had with Jesus in Capernaum. But that will have to wait for another time. Right now he needs to get the facts concerning our imprisonment so that he can use his authority from Rome to end our struggle here in Netzereth."

Slowly the captives, who had moved far away from the two soldiers, relaxed and began to share with Cretius the events of the last week. After an hour of conversations, Cretius announced that he wished to have everyone sit so he could address them all.

"I will start by saying that I am here at the request of James and out of respect for his brother Jesus. I am glad to be in the presence of people who also admire Jesus. But I am also under the authority of Rome and I will do my job faithfully to keep the order that Caesar has asked of me in Galilee. This is what I have gleaned in speaking with you today that is of interest to Rome and the peace we strive to maintain. The authorities of this village have conducted a trial and found a man guilty of murder and have subsequently executed him. The execution was done without the approval of the Roman authorities and therefore illegal. Simon has told me that he foolishly attacked two leaders and in the scuffle one of the men died. Simon has agreed to stand trial for that attack but assures me he was not the one who delivered the deadly blow.

The man, Jesus of Netzereth has ridden into Jerusalem on a donkey to the admiration of a large crowd which believed that action to be his declaration of kingship in Jerusalem. If that is true, that is a major problem. The leadership…or most of the leadership," Cretius made a side glance to Elder Ezra, "have decided to hold all followers of Jesus in case they arise to rebel against Rome on behalf of Jesus. You claim however that the real reason you are being held is so that the Elders might confiscate your land and profit off your arrest and or excommunication."

Cretius paused and looked over the room. "I want to tell you that I find it highly unlikely that Jesus of Netzereth would make a claim of kingship. I don't know your Holy Scriptures as well as you do but, the man I know is of humble demeanor despite his authority in teaching and healing. Therefore, I believe we can take care of things quickly here and set things right for you all."

There was a mental and emotional relief that flowed over the people and smiles and hugs started to flow. Then a loud knock on the doors and the two soldiers at the door burst in.

"Centurion! You need to come hear this!"

Cretius walked to the door and everyone else followed. There in the street stood a Hebrew next to a horse that looked like it had been ridden hard. Next to him was Matthan.

"Centurion!" Matthan said. "This man is a friend of our village who has ridden hard the last two days from Jerusalem with news about what has happened there." He then looked at the messenger and said, "Tell him everything you just told me."

"Sir, I have been riding since the end of Sabbath to get here as soon as possible with news that I knew my brothers in Netzereth would want to have. On the morning of this past sixth day, Pontius Pilate ordered that Jesus of Netzereth be crucified on Golgotha. The authorities hung him on a cross with a notice that read 'This is the King of the Jews'! Jesus died on the cross and was buried before Sabbath."

James received the news from the Jerusalem messenger, and his mouth fell open. The events of the past week had completely changed the way he understood the world. His family had been ripped apart by ideologies and misunderstandings. His friendship with a true companion had been stretched to the limit and then destroyed. His beliefs about his brother had been tested, failed, reborn, and now dashed again. His heart could not take one more vicious stab. It was a wonder that he had any hope left at all. And yet, if he understood the significance it could set things right again. That is, if the message was true to the understanding that Jacob had given him.

But it was the notice on the cross that caught the attention of the Roman soldiers. All eyes were fixed on Cretius.

The Centurion turned and commanded his soldiers, "Shut the doors and keep the prisoners in there. We will have an inquest tomorrow morning to decide what is to be done with them." Then turning to Matthan and the messenger he said, "You two come with me. I have a number of questions."

CHAPTER 17

(Monday Evening)

Nathaniel was tired. He was tired of walking, tired of looking, tired of arguing with the three useless men that had come with him on this hunt for Joseph and Simon. They had walked through the day to reach Cana. They arrived very late, camped and rested outside the village until daybreak on this morning. Then they began their search for the two brothers starting with the cousins of the heretic's family. No one admitted to seeing either Joseph or Simon but Nathaniel left one of the men to keep a watch on the homestead in case the brothers showed up. Then he and the others walked every street of Cana, looked in every public place and house, and surveyed every field around Cana with no success. However, they did succeed in finding the first man they had left at the homestead drunk and yelling accusations at anyone who walked by him. And when Nathaniel tried to sober him up by sticking his big head in a bucket of water at the town well, the drunk's buddies started tearing into Nathaniel. Soon there was a complete fist fight between all four of them and they were thrown out of the village by the citizens who were laughing at them all and ridiculing them for being Netzerites. "Nothing good can come from Netzereth."

Nathaniel left the three to find their own way back to Netzereth and he started his trudge home. Now at sunset he found himself in one of the worst places on earth. Sepphoris was the home of the Magistrate Gaius, a puppet of Herod Antipas and Rome. The whole town smelled of the foul stench of Rome. He wanted to get through the town as quickly as possible and get to Netzereth within two hours time. *This whole search was a complete loss.* He thought. *Hopefully Heber had better luck in Nain.*

He was looking for a well where he could quench his thirst and debating in his own mind if he should drink Sepphoris water when something caught his eye. A boy was kicking a ball in the street ahead of him. He looked familiar. As he walked closer Nathaniel knew it was the son of James.

"He is a friend who lives in the Essene quarter of Jerusalem." Matthan was explaining to Cretius. "As we Netzerim are also of the Essene school of thought, our brothers in Jerusalem keep us informed of major religious happenings in Jerusalem. You can trust that what he is saying is the truth."

Cretius looked at the Jerusalem messenger, "Tell me about the notice that was on the cross."

"It was nailed above his head and it said, 'Jesus of Netzereth King of the Jews'" he replied.

"What else? Was it written just in Aramaic?"

"No sir. It was written in Aramaic, Latin, and Greek. And the soldiers who crucified him also called him 'King of the Jews'... in jest." he added sheepishly.

Cretius thought quietly for a second and then asked, "Are you sure he died before sundown."

"Oh yes! The soldiers knew that there would be a problem if the crucifixion was still being done during Sabbath so they broke the legs of the other two men who were being crucified. But when they got to Jesus he was already dead. They pierced his heart with a spear just to make sure. And then one of our Sanhedrin asked permission from Pilate to bury Jesus in his tomb. Pilate granted permission."

"I knew he was a pretender." Matthan whispered.

Cretius ignored the comment and said, "Well Jesus' crucifixion was obviously carried out in an official manner. The notice in three languages, the method of determining death, and the permission for burial by Pilate all point to an orderly execution."

Matthan sat up straight and began to envision the new Netzereth without the heresy of Jesus to upset the dream of a true Netzer Messiah. And then Cretius dashed his hopes.

"An orderly execution, unlike the one that took place here this morning." Then looking directly at Matthan he said, "What right did you have to execute a convicted murderer without informing the magistrate in Sepphoris of your plans? I will be holding an official inquest tomorrow morning to decide what should be done here."

Cretius left Matthan and returned to the synagogue.

James, Judas, Simon, Ezra, Saul and Gurion sat in a circle together discussing the ramifications of the news from Jerusalem.

Gurion put his hand on James' back, "This is terrible news my friends. I'm so sorry for you and your family. Regardless of his claims. Jesus was your brother. And I weep with you men."

All three brothers nodded their thanks to Gurion. They all knew that they were surrounded by friends at this dark hour. In their sadness they had comfort from family. In their shock they had the support of friends. But even more important was that in their confusion they had knowledge-able people who helped them think through the meaning of Jesus' death.

"What does his death mean? Is it the end of the role of the Netzer? Was he not really the Netzer as we had hoped? Or… is this still part of the Almighty's plan for the Netzer that we have misunderstood or failed to see?" Saul looked at Ezra hoping to get some insight from the scholar of the prophetic texts.

"If Jacob was right," James offered, "this death is in some way a sacrifice to take away our sin. But surely death by Roman crucifixion is not an acceptable sacrifice by sacred law?"

"No, sacrifices must be made in the Temple on the altar and officiated by a priest." Ezra responded.

"But" Judas interrupted, "the Passover lamb was not sacrificed in the Temple while we were slaves in Egypt and its blood on our doorposts was still efficacious. Perhaps the sacrifice of the lamb that takes away the sin of the world need not be done as we would expect. But is there any other indication that The Name would accept such a death. The death of a criminal?"

"But he wasn't a criminal, brother." Simon reacted.

"He was to the Romans if he claimed to be king and started a rebellion."

"NO. I'm a criminal." Simon said forcefully. "I attacked Matthan and Jeremiah which resulted in Jeremiah's death and didn't stop the death of Jacob which I was intending to do. I deserve to die. Jesus never did anything wrong. I can't remember a time I could actually accuse him of doing anything wrong." Then realizing something, Simon looked at James and Judas and continued excitedly. "Our brother Joseph saw it too. Remember we were sitting around the fire the morning before Passover and Joseph was laughing at how often Jesus would do things that we thought would get him in trouble. But he always had the correct view on why he acted the way he did and could convince Father and Mother of his innocence. He has done it again."

The others stared at Simon not knowing what he was getting at.

Simon counted them off on his fingers as he listed the facts. "Jesus stayed behind in Jerusalem because he had to be about his father's business. And our parents agreed. He read Torah to Widow Miriam instead of attending assembly. And our Netzereth leaders agreed. He arranged a marriage for James with a woman who was not a descendent of King David. And Mother and the rest of our family agreed. He moved to Capernaum to start his teaching ministry. And as of late, I believe, we all agree with his move." Simon gave them all a questioning look. They all hesitantly nodded assent. "He's done it again. He has done something which we see as foolish, absurd, and even criminal. And yet," Simon's smile grew large, "I bet you he will come out the winner somehow."

All six men sat in silence and mulled over the revelation Simon had just shared and one by one all of them began chuckling and then laughing out loud. Others in the assembly room looked at them and began smiling as well. Joy once again filled the room and a new spirit of hope, trust, and belief in the Netzer Messiah overtook them all.

"Okay, okay." Ezra rose from his seat in excitement. "I have an idea. Remember Judas when we were reading in Isaiah about the suffering servant?" Judas nodded. "I think there might be a death reversal coming. The passage said something about life after death. Come with me all of you let's go get the scroll and read it again."

Ezra almost ran to the scriptorium with a large group of people following him. He soon emerged excitedly fighting his way to the bema and unrolled the scroll. As he looked for the right passage everyone gathered around to hear what had excited their Elder so much. He finally found the passage and motioned everyone to be quiet and then read slowly and emphatically...

For he was cut off from the land of the living: for the transgression of my people he was punished. He was assigned a grave with the wicked, and with the rich in his death, though he had done no violence, nor was any deceit in his mouth. Yet it was the Lord's will to crush him and cause him to suffer, and though the Lord makes his life an offering for sin, he will see his offspring and prolong his days, and the will of the Lord will prosper his hand. After he has suffered, he will see the light of life and be satisfied; by his knowledge my righteous servant will justify many, and he will bear their iniquities.

The brothers raised their hands in excitement and the room erupted in applause.

Hadassah came out of the room and called for Joshua. There was no response. She looked in all the corners of the courtyard. Nothing. She searched the roof tops of the inn. No one. She knocked on the door of the innkeeper and he answered.

"Excuse me; I can't seem to find my son. Have you seen him?"

"No. Wasn't he with you?"

"Yes he was in our room with us when we all laid down for a nap but the rest of us overslept. He must have gotten up and stepped out to play in the courtyard."

"Oh yes. I did see him briefly. He was playing with a ball by the fire pit but that was at sunset hours ago."

Just then Joseph and Zerah walked into the courtyard from the street.

"Joseph," Hadassah yelled, "is Joshua with you?"

"No, the last time I saw him he was going with you into the room for a nap."

Hadassah looked at him with motherly worry.

"I'll go search the nearby streets and homes. You ladies check again in here."

"There are no other guests." The innkeeper said. "You may look in the other rooms."

Zerah and Hadassah quickly started searching the three other rooms. Soon Emma was up and searching also while holding tight to Sarah. Then Joseph walked in slowly reading a piece of paper.

"What is that?" Hadassah asked running to his side.

"It's bad. Matthan has him." He handed the note to Hadassah and continued. "I found the note on the outside of the courtyard gate. They want me and Simon to come back to Netzereth."

Hadassah read the note through tears. She screamed and Emma and Zerah came to comfort her. Then she threw the note down and yelled, "I'm going to Netzereth to get my son."

Five minutes later all five of them were on their way back to Netzereth. Joseph knew there was no way he would have been able to convince any of them to stay safely in Sepphoris. He silently prayed that James' plan to bring the Romans to Netzereth had worked.

CHAPTER 18

(Tuesday Morning)

Cretius and his men had set up camp on the half-finished porch of the synagogue to act as a buffer between the followers of Jesus inside and the other townspeople outside. When Nathaniel had entered Netzereth with Joshua in tow and saw the Roman soldiers, he took the boy to Matthan's home. Matthan would have preferred to keep the child overnight but his incessant whimpering, and Matthan's desire to be well rested for the morning activities, convinced him to take the child to the synagogue. As he left the porch of the synagogue Matthan could hear the shouts of joy coming from inside and his irritation with the heretics grew.

James and Hadassah sat awake in the early morning watching their family sleep. Joseph and the rest of the family had arrived during the night obviously worried but then rejoicing to see Joshua safe and well.

"I'm surprised at how Emma reacted to the news of Jacob's death." James said to his wife as he stroked her hand.

Hadassah nodded, "She is a rock. The report you gave her of her husband's testimony for the Netzer encouraged her. But I think her sadder emotions will hit her later today during the inquest. How did you find a Centurion who is sympathetic to Jesus?"

James shook his head, "I don't know. The timing was perfect. The day I arrived, the Magistrate was out of town. But I spoke with the Physician's head servant who knows this Centurion who happens to be in Sepphoris for the day. It is like the accounts in the Torah where everything is going awful and the Almighty orchestrates a deliverance."

"Yes, like Joseph, sold into slavery, wrongly accused, thrown into prison, meeting the servants of Pharaoh, interpreting their dreams and then Pharaoh's dream thus saving Egypt and his family. Everything is going wrong and The One puts all the pieces in place for a miraculous deliverance. Is that what we are experiencing?" Hadassah's excitement grew and she had to be shushed by nearby adults wanting their children to stay asleep.

"It sure seems that way dear. But even beyond our story here, I think there is a grander story being played out in Jerusalem." He looked at his wife with a smile. She smiled back and they embraced.

"Hey, you two, cut that out. This is a public place. You are making a spectacle of yourselves." Judas snickered behind them still lying on his pillow. James picked up his pillow and threw it at Judas. And the three of them had to stifle their laughter.

Then Zerah who was lying nearby let out a big sigh. Hadassah turned to her and asked, "Are you okay Zerah?"

Zerah rose to a sitting position, pushed her dark hair out of her eyes and responded. "I don't understand how you all can be so comfortable. I'm nervous. We have been in hiding because staying in Netzereth was unsafe. Now we are back here and Roman soldiers are going to decide our fate this morning. Just the fact that our enemies were willing to steal a child from his mother yesterday should put some caution in us all."

The three of them looked at Zerah and nodded, and then looked at each other and smiled and snickered. "I don't get it either Zerah." James said. "There is just something in the air that causes me to sing and laugh and praise the Almighty for His goodness. I can't explain it. Maybe we should be worried but I can't be worried when I think about my brother the Netzer fulfilling his mission. Maybe it is because we know Jesus better than you. How much time did you spend with Jesus when he was living here in Netzereth?"

"Not much time. He left here when I was eleven. I remember sometimes he would be sitting at the well and we would listen to him tell stories. He had quite an imagination. He would talk about rich men and their servants, farmers and their crops. Oh, this one story he told was about a woman which he named Hadassah."

"Oh, do tell us that story." Hadassah said while shaking Zerah's leg under her blanket.

"Well, it seems Hadassah had a coin purse with ten silver coins in it. One day she counted the coins and only had nine. So, she moved everything out of her house swept the floor, walls, and ceiling looking for the coin. She eventually found it and then invited all her friends and neighbors over for a celebration saying 'Rejoice with me. I have found my lost coin.'"

Everyone turned and looked at Hadassah.

"Well see, he didn't have such a great imagination." They continued to look at her. "And they were copper coins and I only invited Emma over to celebrate." Hadassah acted indignant, and then smiled, and broke out laughing. "But I did move all the furniture out of the house and sweep the ceiling." She laughed. And then louder "And Jesus helped me."

Now they were all laughing. And no one was sleeping anymore.

Matthan woke with a start! The knock at his door was louder the second time followed by a voice calling to him. "Rabbi Matthan!"

He quickly rose and threw a robe around himself. "Just a minute please."

At the door was Elder Akim. "Rabbi, I have just received some important news."

Matthan pushed past him and motioned for Akim to follow. He led him out of the room used for sleeping through the courtyard to the room used for eating and teaching. Once inside, Matthan pulled a chair out for Akim and poured two glasses of water for them before speaking. "What is this important news?" He said as he lowered himself into his chair and took a long drink of water.

"I have just heard from travelers to Netzereth that the cohort of Roman soldiers we thought were coming to our village to arrest the followers of Jesus have passed us by and have continued on the Way of the Sea to the capital at Tiberius."

Matthan stared at his glass and said, "So?"

"Doesn't that mean that they were never on their way here? That they were not seeking out the followers of Jesus? That the whole reason for our fretting and frustration over the 'Triumphant Entry' into Jerusalem was unnecessary? We didn't need to have that meeting where Jacob killed our Rabbi. We didn't need to put Jacob on trial and execute him. We didn't need to confine the followers of Jesus in the synagogue. We didn't need to have Romans here to defile our place of worship." With each statement Akim's voice got louder and more accusatory.

Matthan placed his glass on the table, sighed and folded his arms in front of him resting them on the table. He then slowly raised his head and looked at Akim. "The road behind us is always clearer than the road ahead of us. We are where we are. And we must deal wisely and according to Scripture in our actions now. This is what we know now. The heretic Jesus is still a heretic leading some of our Netzerim brothers astray. He has claimed to be the king of the Jews, attested by

Pilate himself. Romans are in our village and want to hear our arguments for the actions we have taken. Jacob killed our Rabbi Isaiah and deserved to die, 'eye for eye, life for life' according to the Law of Moses. Those still in the synagogue have not yet renounced their belief that Jesus is the Netzer. They must be removed from our midst or they will continue to corrupt our village and children." He paused to let the truth sink in to Akim's mind. "At the inquest this morning I will argue for the lawful execution of Jacob under the Law of Moses and request the removal of those who follow Jesus because they are enemies of Caesar."

Matthan stood and walked to the door. "Elder Akim, I suggest you assemble the rest of the elders and prepare them for the inquest." Matthan exited leaving the door open for Akim who sat alone.

The inquest was held on the porch of the synagogue as a number of people complained about the Romans being in the assembly room. The doors and front windows were open wide so that the followers of Jesus could hear the proceedings. Two of Cretius' men stood on the porch next to a table behind which sat Cretius and Janus. Janus would serve as the scribe for the inquest. The rest of the village, or those who wished to show up and be in the presence of Romans, stood in the street in front of the synagogue.

"The first issue," Cretius began, "is the trial and execution of Jacob. In particular the execution which took place without Roman authority. Is there someone in the synagogue who wishes to speak to this issue?"

"I do." Judas took one step out of the door and faced Cretius.

"Proceed." Cretius commanded.

"My brother Simon and I were there at the execution. We wanted to stop it and tried to do so by speaking to the men about what Simon learned outside of Matthan's house the night before. We now know that the execution of Jacob and the excommunication of the followers of Jesus was an attempt by a few men to profit off the turmoil of the village. We also know that Jacob did not kill Isaiah but the evidence was tampered with and false witnesses were brought forth to convict Jacob. Jacob should not have been executed at all and definitely not outside of Roman law." Judas stepped back into the meeting room.

Cretius whispered a question to his scribe and received a nod from him. He then looked out at the street and asked, "Is there someone who wishes to speak from the leadership of Netzereth?"

"Yes, I will." Responded Matthan. "I have heard that there is a Roman Centurion stationed in Capernaum who has taken an interest in the beliefs of the Jews. In fact, he funded the building of their new synagogue. Is that you sir?"

"Yes, that would be me."

"Well, as a man who respects the Jewish people and their beliefs I am sure you are aware that our law requires an 'eye for an eye'. We were fulfilling the Law of Moses during a time when it would have been dangerous for us to report to the Magistrate in Sepphoris given the claims of the imposter Jesus. We ask for your grace in this matter seeing as we fulfilled the laws of our Holy Scriptures. As to the claim that it was not a fair trial," Matthan waved his hand as if shooing an insignificant insect, "there is no evidence of such. The testimony of Judas to suggest otherwise did not have corroborating witnesses. And since he has brought up the issue of Simon's attack on me the night before, let me add that Simon should be placed under arrest for the murder of Jeremiah who was our head elder at the time."

"Interesting points made by both sides." Cretius closed his eyes in thought and awaited his scribe to indicate he had recorded the pertinent information. "I have decided to accept the words of Matthan that the trial of Jacob was necessary and carried out correctly. And although I see dangerous precedent being set in this I will overlook the execution of Jacob because of the respect I have for the Jewish Scripture and people."

Matthan smiled and nodded. Things were going well.

Inside the synagogue there was an audible sigh from many people and Emma who had been sitting just in earshot began to weep openly. Hadassah and a few other women moved to her side to comfort her.

"As to the issue of Simon and his attack of Matthan's home." Cretius continued, "Simon has already confessed to me and placed himself in my custody. He claims that it was you Matthan, who struck the fatal blow to Jeremiah. You claim it was him. Based on the same Law of Moses which we both hold as so important I can't convict either of you of Jeremiah's death because convictions are to be on the basis of two or more witnesses. Therefore, Simon will be taken to Capernaum and judged there by the magistrate. I will recommend that he serve a sentence of two years labor for my household for the attack on you Matthan."

James looked at Simon and smiled. Simon smiled back knowing that he would learn much more about blacksmithing in a Roman household, and two years would be an easy price to pay.

Matthan frowned and turned in disgust. He did not expect that verdict.

Cretius continued, "Now as to the incarceration of the followers of Jesus, is there someone who wishes to speak for those in the synagogue?"

"I will speak for the followers of the True Netzer." Elder Ezra stepped out of the door.

A rumbling of voices moved through the crowd in the street. They were silenced by Cretius' outstretched arm and the movement of the standing soldiers' hands to their sword hilts. Cretius nodded to Ezra.

"In the beginning the separation of us from the others was legitimately a move to protect both sides from physical harm and I... we all appreciate the concern shown as both sides were enraged by the events of the week. The incarceration was then transformed, after the unfortunate death of Rabbi Isaiah, into a desire to rid Netzereth of those who held on to the once prominent view that Jesus Ben Joseph was the Netzer Messiah. A view that I am ashamed to say even I abandoned for a time. Most in Netzereth no longer believe him to be the Netzer because of his affiliation with the Pharisee sect and his teachings about Gentiles. Those who still believed became a small minority who were tolerated because of kinship. However, it soon became clear that there were some in our village who wished to destroy Jesus followers' place in the village for financial and personal gain. We know that former Elder Jeremiah was actively seeking to gain my land by my excommunication and wanted to cancel the marriage contract of Joseph, brother of James so that he could marry Zerah, the daughter of David. These things we know and have evidence to prove them."

"What evidence?" shouted Matthan.

"First," replied Ezra, "there is the conversation that Simon overheard outside your home before he attacked you."

"Again, the unsubstantiated claim of one person. There must be two witnesses."

"The second witness is the written document with Jeremiah's signature that I have here in my hand." Matthan turned around to see Elder Akim holding up a parchment and behind him stood David.

Cretius motioned for one of his men to retrieve the parchment. He brought it back to Cretius who quickly read it.

"This document says that Jeremiah was offering the family of David half of the land formerly owned by Ezra in exchange for the promise of marriage to his daughter Zerah." Cretius put the document on the table, slid it to his scribe, and looked at David and Akim. "Do you two testify that this was a legitimate offer by Jeremiah?"

"I do." replied Akim.

"I do." David hesitantly replied.

"Thank you. Is there someone who wishes to speak for the leaders about the issue of the incarceration of the followers of Jesus?" Cretius looked at Matthan.

"I must remind you sir that Jesus claimed to be king of the Jews. Pilate himself had the inscription written and placed on the cross. These followers are traitors to Rome and follow a usurping king. You must meet out punishment for their traitorous ways."

Cretius looked at his scribe to make sure everything was recorded properly and then stood. "Based on the evidence, I have decided that there have been grievous sins committed by the leadership of Netzereth against some of the people of their own village. I will take the evidence to the magistrate in Capernaum for his decision. However, I am ordering that all citizens of Netzereth be released to their homes immediately as the threat of Jesus as King of the Jews was handled by Jerusalem courts. As Jesus is dead, there is now no king for these people to follow, if indeed they ever really had designs to do so. If it is argued that believing Jesus to be the Netzer is the same as treason against Caesar, then I must arrest all of you, for all of you believe that your God will be sending a messiah to save you from the Gentiles. Do you not?"

There was no response.

Two hours later in their family home James, Joseph, Judas, Hadassah, and the children said goodbye to Simon with hugs and kisses. James turned to Cretius and said, "Thank you friend. You are always welcome in my home. You are a man of honor, and I am indebted to you. Please take good care of my brother."

"James, I expect you to visit him often. I want to hear more stories about your brother Jesus. I am saddened by his death."

James nodded and bowed his head. Cretius mounted his horse and led his troop and Simon out of the courtyard and eventually out of Netzereth.

Hadassah stepped up to James' side and said, "Simon will tell him some stories about your brother that will entertain him." Then she tugged at his sleeve and said, "Come on let's go help the others."

By 'others' she meant those who had gone to the base of the cliff to retrieve the body of Jacob and give him a proper burial. They began to exit when they were stopped by Elder Akim.

"I'm glad I caught you James. I expect you are going to help get Jacob's body ready for burial?"

"Yes we are on our way now. Why did you want to see me? And thanks for your help today at the inquest. Ezra thought you would come through but I had my doubts you could convince David to do the right thing. Thank you so much."

"James, I am so sorry for the part I played in making this week so miserable for you. I was confused and fooled by those I trusted. Please accept my sincerest apology."

"Of course, Akim."

"Before you go, I have one other piece of news for you. The Elders have met and decided that Matthan can no longer be trusted to be our rabbi. We have removed him from that position and have asked Ezra to temporarily fill the need."

"How did that go over with Matthan? James asked.

"Not so well. We allowed him to keep the home he is living in but I suspect he will desire to move elsewhere and spread his misery in some other place." Akim snickered. "But please, I have kept you too long. Please go help your friend."

"Thank you again Akim."

James looked up towards the courtyard gate to start his walk to the execution site when suddenly two large horses galloped into the courtyard. And there seated on the horses were Caleb, Hadassah's brother from Nain, and Jesse.

"James. James." Jesse screamed. And then seeing the others he screamed again. "Judas, Joseph, Hadassah, Joshua, Come here quick. He's alive. I've seen him. He's alive He was crucified but now he's alive. The Passover Lamb lives!"

EPILOGUE

James woke with a start. He listened quietly and intently. After a few moments the knock came again and James rose carefully so as to not wake the rest of the family. The importance of the knock was evident from the hour at which it came, but its meaning was a bit frightening.

"Ezra, have you news from Jerusalem?" He spoke softly as he approached the front gate. No answer.

New fears raced through his brain. "Matthan, it's over. Leave my family alone." Still no answer.

A pause, and then the rapping on the front gate again only louder than before. James let a different and even more dangerous possibility play through his thoughts. Perhaps the Romans were aware and furious about the resurrection. Perhaps the stir of activity among the few followers of Jesus was viewed as an attempt of zealots to overthrow the authority structure. Outside the gate may be a squadron sent to Netzereth to round up the family of Jesus. But then he realized that it was unlikely that Roman soldiers would be knocking.

James hesitated an arm's length from the gate. Who could it be? Is this the beginning of a new trial or another chapter of the same litigation? The struggles and pains of the past week had turned to excitement and joy with a newfound belief in Jesus. He had just realized that he could count the trials of the past as joy. The trials produced perseverance in his faith in his brother. And he saw the maturity the trial had created in him. But still another trial would be hard to endure so soon.

"Abba Father, give me peace in this hour." James prayed. "Who is there?" he said, somewhat louder than he intended.

"James, open the door and I will come in and give you what you ask."

The voice! It had been quite a while but the attractive kindness was still there and now it also sang with a confident authority. James quickly swung the gate wide.

"Jesus, My brother!" James was about to throw his arms around him when he suddenly realized the magnitude of the encounter and he fell at Jesus' feet. "My Lord. You are the Lamb who takes away the sin of the world!" He stayed there for what seemed to be minutes but in reality was only a few seconds when Jesus reached down and drew him up by the shoulders.

When they stood face to face Jesus gave James a bear hug and spoke softly. "I have so desired for this moment, brother. Receive the peace of my Father."

The rest of the world disappeared in a flood of peace and love, and James caught a glimpse of heaven. There was a sweet fragrance in Jesus' hair which flooded James' mind with remembrances of the love that Jesus had always shown him as his brother. When Jesus released his embrace, James dripped with peace and love. Tears of joy fell from his eyes and stuck in his beard. A smile broke out on his face and Jesus kissed him on both cheeks. They stared at each other, lost in thoughts of their childhood together. And then James' thoughts turned to the times he had ridiculed Jesus' ministry, of coming to save him from himself, and his eyes looked away from the eyes of Jesus.

"James, all is forgiven. You have been redeemed. No more fears, brother. No more shame." Then turning and walking to the still unfinished pillar that rose from the dust in the corner of the courtyard Jesus placed his hands on it. He ran his fingers over the intricate detail James had painstaking etched into the stone. He said, "James I once taught you to make wonderful pillars that would stand the test of time. I now have a new assignment for you. I need you to be a pillar for my church in Jerusalem. Days of trial are coming and they need a servant who knows how to stand strong in the face of overwhelming odds by believing when they can not see. You believed without seeing. You are my pillar. I am sending you."

THE BEGINNING

CHARACTERS OF INTEREST

In order of appearance and chapter

INTRO

James—Brother of Jesus Christ, second son of Joseph and Mary, Netzereth stonemason.

CHAPTER ONE

Hadassah—Wife of James, mother of Joshua and Sarah.
Sarah—One year old daughter of James and Hadassah.
Joshua—Five-year-old son of James and Hadassah.
Emma—Hadassah's best friend in Netzereth, wife of Jacob, mother of Jesse, ardent believer in Jesus.
Jacob—Emma's husband, father of Jesse, friend of James' family, tailor and owner of textile store in Netzereth, ardent believer in Jesus.

Jesse—Twelve-year-old son of Jacob and Emma.

Joseph—Brother of James, third son of Joseph and Mary, stonemason apprentice to James.

Judas—Brother of James, fourth son of Joseph and Mary, scribe apprentice in Netzereth synagogue.

Simon—Brother of James, fifth son of Joseph and Mary, blacksmith apprentice.

Zerah—Betrothed to Joseph, daughter of David.

Isaiah—Head Rabbi of Netzereth

Matthan—New apprentice of Isaiah from the Essene school at Qumran.

CHAPTER TWO

Nathaniel—Jonas' son who has just returned from Jerusalem with important news.

Ezra—Elder of Netzereth

Jeremiah—Head elder of Netzereth.

CHAPTER THREE

No new characters

CHAPTER FOUR

Saul Ben Daniel—Official village crier.

CHAPTER FIVE

Heber—Qumran School classmate and friend of Matthan, one of the "leftovers"
Nathaniel—One of the "leftovers", friend of Matthan.

CHAPTER SIX

No new characters

CHAPTER SEVEN

Gurion—Resident of Netzereth.
Saul—Resident of Netzereth, Believer in Jesus as Netzer.

CHAPTER EIGHT

No new characters

CHAPTER NINE

No new characters

CHAPTER TEN

Johanan—Hadassah's father, Resident of Nain.

CHAPTER ELEVEN

Caleb—Brother of Hadassah, Eldest son of Johanan.

Deborah—Wife of Micah, Sister of Seth, the man Jesus raised to life in Nain.

CHAPTER TWELVE

Josiah—Resident of Netzereth.

Hazael—Resident of Netzereth.

Tomas—Resident of Netzereth.

Jonas—Resident of Netzereth, Father of Jacob.

Elder Joseph—Elder of Netzereth.

CHAPTER THIRTEEN

Nathan—Resident of Netzereth, Believer in Jesus as Netzer.

Benjamin—Resident of Netzereth, Guard in synagogue.

CHAPTER FOURTEEN

No new characters

CHAPTER FIFTEEN

Akim—Elder in Netzereth.

Elizabeth—Servant of the Greek Doctor, Heretas, in Sepphoris.

Rachael—Servant of the Greek Doctor, Heretas, in Sepphoris.

Petros—Head Servant of the Greek Doctor, Heretas, in Sepphoris.
Antony—Brother of Petros, Servant of Roman Centurion Cretius.
Heretas—Greek physician to the Roman Magistrate, Gaius.
Cretius—Roman Centurion in Capernaum who asked Jesus
    to heal his servant.

CHAPTER SIXTEEN

Janus—Roman soldier under Cretius' command.

CHAPTER SEVENTEEN

No new characters

CHAPTER EIGHTEEN

No new characters